Welles-Turner
Memorial Library
Glastonbury, CT 06033

D1252572

DISCARDED BY
WELLES-TURNER
MEMORIAL LIBRARY
GLASTONBURY, CT

This book was purchased
with funds from the
Cornelia H. Nearing Endowment

SPIRITS
SUGAR
WATER
BITTERS

HOW THE COCKTAIL CONQUERED THE WORLD

SPIRITS
SUGAR
WATER
BITTERS

HOW THE COCKTAIL CONQUERED THE WORLD

Derek Brown
with Robert Yule

Get ready to be educated, enlightened, and entertained! Mixologist Derek Brown is about to take you on a romp through the history of the cocktail—a purely American invention—told in the context of our long love affair with alcohol.

And Brown knows his history! He served as our Chief Spirits Advisor in 2015 when the National Archives Foundation launched Spirited Republic: Alcohol's Evolving Role in U.S. History, an exhibit that explored the role the federal government has played in regulating, promoting, investigating, prohibiting, and warning about alcohol. In a series of associated seminars, he brought the cocktail out of the dark ages to delighted packed audiences. The romp begins nearly ten thousand years ago in a village in China with fermented drink of rice, honey, and hawthorn fruit. A self-proclaimed student of anthropology with a love of the vast human history, Brown documents the fact that drinking alcohol existed in the Americas before the arrival of the Europeans and that an Aztec alcoholic beverage contained the rinds of pineapples and spices.

The real fun begins with his research on our Founding Drinkers. Did you know that Spanish sherry was the base for a mixture of sugar and citrus served over crushed ice? Or that beer was key to the survival of the colonists who were notoriously suspicious of the local water? And that our first settlers found the land "so full of grapes" that the first American wines were born? By the mid-1700s, drinking was so pervasive that Benjamin Franklin was able to publish The Drinkers Dictionary, a list of more than two hundreds ways of describing how to get drunk!

Ten chapters tell the colorful history of the cocktail. You will learn about how the Old Fashioned became the king of American spirits in the 1800s, the importance of ice in the cocktail's history, the evolution of bartenders and drinkers over time, and the birth of the classic cocktails. While the temperance movement and Prohibition disrupted access, Brown documents how even in the nation's capital, the cocktail survived—and thrived. The resurgence of the cocktail beginning in the 1980s and '90s with the Cosmopolitan and flavored vodkas transformed mixology and cocktail appreciation. Mixologists with an eye to the past trace the history of the classics in the creation of new classics, enriching our knowledge and appreciation for the role the cocktail has played in our history. As Brown has said, a cocktail "is complex and articulates a story with its history, its ingredients, and the person who made it. It's not just about drinking, but what we're drinking and where it's from."

Along the way you will learn a lot about Derek Brown and also about the rise of the cocktail nerd. The book ends with a "history of the present" in which Brown shares his personal journey and his dedication to becoming the best bartender in the world. His pledge to his readers—"Drinkers of the world: You are our people, and we are yours."

And the best part of the book? Forty-five cocktail recipes, including General's Orders, a rye whiskey drink Brown created for our Spirited Republic exhibit.

So grab your shaker and get ready to celebrate another ingenious American invention—the cocktail!

— The Honorable David S. Ferriero,
ARCHIVIST OF THE UNITED STATES

Writing this book was cathartic for me. For more than a decade, I have lived in a semi-insular world of cocktails, cocktail bars, and cocktail personalities. That world's drinks, places, and legends have defined my life in a way that is rightly called "the craft bartender lifestyle." And now I get to share that world with you, for better or worse.

If the most famous bartender in the world walked down the street, I doubt that anyone would recognize her. That is more than a little humbling, especially for someone like me who hasn't approached that status. To further put it in perspective, one Yelp review questioned my bartending skills and asked, "What does he think he is, some kind of professor? He just pours things from a large container into a smaller one." Touché. That is, in essence, what I did. But I have a retort.

In 2009, I was invited to the White House to make drinks for the president and senior staff. In 2015, I was named the Chief Spirits Advisor to the National Archives Foundation, from which this book was spawned. Not only are those notable events, but they are humbling in an entirely different way—they show that people are taking craft bartending and cocktails seriously. In fact, when I met President Obama, I was introduced to him as "the mixologist." He turned to me and said, "Isn't that just a bartender?" I was initially crestfallen and he must have sensed it. He smiled and added, "Well, being a bartender is a lot like being a coach"—as he pointed to Michelle—"or being president. Everyone thinks they can do it, but they can't, can they?" No, they can't. So, as much as I admire iconic cocktail writer David Embury's sentiment that anyone can make great cocktails, or as much as I jest about the tiny fame associated with craft bartenders and their drinks, I have some truly serious things to say. Without this insular life and the various drinks, places, and people contained therein, I would not have found a home, my purpose, or had much fun at all. At one point being a bartender was all I wanted to be. It's a damn respectable profession and one that I will always admire. To all the bartenders out there, and to all the people I could not or did not include in these chapters, please accept my most humble apology. I was grateful to be included for a time in your midst, one of the "stalwarts of the siphon"—a bartender, mixologist, or whatever the hell you want to call it.

The quote "America's business is business" has won recognition, but I would replace it with "America's business is drinking," a business we take very seriously. So seriously that at the founding of our republic, Americans yearly drank 7.1 gallons of pure alcohol. When I was named Chief Spirits Advisor at the National Archives, a job that I joke makes me the highest-ranking bartender in the U.S. government (though no such rank exists), my first question was, "How can we include cocktails?" So we created a series of ten seminars and invited the top bartenders, cocktail personalities, spirit makers, and cocktail and spirit writers and journalists to join us. None of them were paid to attend—they did so as their patriotic duty. This amazing series, ranging from "Before the Cocktail" to the "Platinum Age," was attended by hundreds of people, though only a few people attended all ten of them. I was one of those people, for obvious reasons. My co-author Bob was another.

It is a little sad that we did not capture the series on audio or film. There was so much information, and it was really, really great. You will have to take my word on it, as this book is not a faithful retelling of the series. However, it is my faithful retelling of what I learned, both at the series and throughout my time as a bartender. In that way, it is not a complete story either. I stepped out from behind the bar, and the bar world has continued to evolve and grow. One hundred years from now, what we know may be upended and retold so very differently. I welcome that. Far from trying to be the definitive historian filling in every detail, place, and person, I just imagined that I was talking to you over a bar. The stories and ideas conveyed in this book are meant to be shared drink in hand. So if you have not yet poured yourself a drink, might I suggest you start with a cold bottle of Manzanilla sherry, a dry fortified wine from southwestern Spain? The book starts and ends with sherry for a very good reason. As you'll learn, sherry was among the first new drinks to reach the Americas, and is one of the classic cocktail ingredients now experiencing a slow resurgence.

Throughout the book I hope you will find very good reasons to drink. At the end of every chapter I have included four classic or new classic drinks and one of my own recipes. This mirrors the way I have always liked to create cocktails: Start with the classics; make up your own seldomly. (Creativity can be its own vice and the classics have attained their status for a reason.) But maybe you want to veer off course a little and make your own cocktails. I get it—it's fun. So that's why sometimes I mention that particular cocktails are easy to switch around this or that ingredient.

Just one last thing before you enter these pages: a plea for understanding the bartender as an unsung force of history—the hand that pours the drink has also steered the ship more often than one might think. (If not for any other reason than the captain was drunk and the bartender was the only one left sober. Just kidding.) The saloon-keep, bartender, or mixologist has provided humanity with the same service that was once reserved for shamans, alchemists, and wizards—they have helped heal, transform, and dazzle us. And, after you read this book and head down to your local cocktail bar asking for such-and-such cocktail, please, for heaven's sake, tip your bartender.

INTRODUCTION

B.C.   BEFORE THE COCKTAIL

B.C. > 1490

THE REAL OLDEST PROFESSION

Alcohol doesn't really need us: it already exists in nature. In fact, for alcohol to exist, all it needs is sugar and yeast. The sugars can come from a ripe fruit and the yeast from the skin of that fruit. These wild yeasts, called saccharomyces, consume the fruit sugars and expel both ethanol (the only potable kind of alcohol for humans) and carbon dioxide. In other words, take a ripe fruit and a little yeast—*et voilà*—nature makes a mixed drink, of sorts. In this way, nature is her own liquor cabinet.

Let's say that this fruit was a peach and that the fermented proto-cocktail would then be a prehistoric Bellini, a fizzy, peachy, and delicious drink originally created in Italy by Giuseppe Cipriani from white peach puree and the Italian sparkling wine Prosecco. Here, nature does her handiwork sans bartender (sorry, Giuseppe). So nature tends bar too. However, if that were the end, this would be a very short book indeed. It turns out that the story of humanity is awash in booze, as well as more than a few early mixologists.

Alcohol has pretty much been with us from the very beginning of mankind, though we possessed neither the skills to write down the date the first drink was made, nor the foresight to keep a stash aside of that very first vintage. (Who would have the patience to wait for nearly 300,000 years to drink it anyway?) Some anthropologists even think that alcohol was a progenitor of certain crucial human endeavors and at the very heart of our artistic and spiritual development, becoming the impetus for forms of symbolic thought among prehuman hominid species. It's easy, in a way, to imagine Neanderthals having a tipple or two before stenciling their hands on the wall or drawing images dancing in the flickering light of the fire, reminiscent of some artsy desert rave.

Regardless, we do know that alcohol evolved hand in hand with civilization, and that the "Fertile Crescent" may well have been the "Fruitive Cup." Some archaeologists argue that creating alcohol, not bread, was the true purpose of agriculture. Makes sense to me: I love a loaf of bread as much as the next guy, but I'd prefer a stiff drink. Even now, alcohol is a jewel in the crown of civilization and ubiquitous in many people's lives, no matter where they live. We celebrate with it, console ourselves with it, cheer our friends and achievements with it, build rituals around it, and, sometimes, just plain let loose with it. To paraphrase Homer (Simpson, not the Greek poet), it's both a problem and a solution. Even if we don't technically need alcohol, it sure seems to be a popular accessory.

If alcohol doesn't need people and, in her own way, nature operates as the saloon, the first drinkers didn't need us either—"us" meaning bartenders. Since the molecules in alcohol are light and easily dispersed in the air, that theoretical first "drink"—the prehistoric Bellini—would have attracted certain animals after it had dropped from the tree and lay there on the forest floor with its wafting aromas. There's a body of evidence that certain genetic qualities we share with small primates, such as aye-ayes, who long past branched off from our ancestral tree, show that we both evolved to consume alcohol. So, we have the first drink and the first drinker—a small arboreal primate sipping on a prehistoric Bellini—but still not a bartender in sight.

Yet, it goes without saying that bartenders have vastly improved alcohol and, in that way, we've made an indelible mark on civilization. Our shining achievement is the cocktail itself. We'll get to that, but my point is that this isn't a fad. Since those early days, humans drank, but we also mixed alcohol in surprising and inventive ways. We're not just talking about primitive, fermented drinks such as beer or wine, but complex drinks that involved multiple fermented beverages, plants, fruits, berries, herbs, spices, and various botanicals. Mankind's so-called oldest profession may well be assigned to ignoble means, but I've always suspected that it took some early hominid "barkeep" to set the mood. We may not know the first barkeep but we do know his or her work.

THE FIRST MIXED DRINK

Every year, about 20,000 of the world's top drinkers gather in New Orleans for a conference called Tales of the Cocktail. (Actually, the world's top bartenders, spirits industry professionals, and enthusiasts. But, yeah, drinkers too.) In 2013, I gave a seminar called "Paleococktails," exploring the earliest recorded mixed drinks and showing how Mesoamerica contributed to this history. Prominent cocktail historian David Wondrich had already taken on the nineteenth century onward, so I had to go very, very early to find my niche. I invited some of the top thinkers on the subject: David Suro-Piñera, director of the Tequila Interchange Project; Dan Healan, anthropologist at Tulane University; Dr. Rodolfo Fernandez, anthropologist at the University of Guadalajara; and Patrick McGovern, a biomolecular archaeologist from Penn State, and also the person who chemically authenticated the earliest discovered alcohol: a fermented drink of rice, honey, and hawthorn fruit. It dated back to circa 7000–6600 BCE (or about ten thousand years ago), and was found in Jiahu, China, a Neolithic village in the Yellow River Valley.

In one of the most striking exchanges, I asked Patrick if that earliest chemically authenticated alcohol was in fact a mixed drink. He answered, unequivocally, yes, confirming for me that some of the first prehistoric drinks were not just singular fermented drinks such as wine or beer. It represents a surprising prelude to the creativity in drinks we see today. That nugget is important because it may suggest why cocktails exist in the space they do, why they garner the kind of experimentation we see at hearths and in kitchens, and why, despite being liquid, they straddle a line between food-like nourishment and something entirely different.

Certainly, humans in antiquity drank straight wine. But it was also common to mix wine with water, barley, honey, resin (as a preservative), or even cheese. Yes, cheese. An example, though showing up much later in antiquity, comes from the eleventh rhapsody of Homer's *Iliad* and provides us with an idea of how these foodstuffs might have made their way into wine: "In it the woman, like unto the goddesses, had mixed for them Pramnian wine, and grated over it a goat's-milk cheese with a brazen rasp, and sprinkled white flour upon it: then bade them drink, as soon as she had prepared the potion." Thankfully for all of us, cheese is rare in both historic and modern mixology.

When it came to mixed drinks, beer wasn't remarkably different. It is commonly thought of as the first beverage. In *The Journal of Archaeological Method and Theory*, authors Brian Hayden, Neil Canuel, and Jennifer Shanse describe how traditional beers might have looked:

> ... beers made in traditional tribal or village societies [in the upper-Neolithic] generally are quite different from modern industrial beers ... traditional beers often have quite low alcohol contents (2–4 percent), include lactic acid fermentation giving them a tangy and sour taste, contain various additives such as honey or fruits, and vary in viscosity from clear liquids, to soupy mixtures with suspended solids, to pastes.

Again, this is essentially closer to a mixed drink, where a multitude of ingredients are used and not just fermented grapes or grains and hops. We're talking about drinks that include sweet, sour, and bitter agents and have a range of presentations. As we bear down upon the invention of the cocktail itself, this will show in part how they connect.

THE FIRST AMERICAN DRINK

Now, drinking alcohol already existed in the Americas before the arrival of Europeans. Early Americans drank pulque, a slightly acidic, milky substance made from agave plants, similar to a beer, which comes in around 3–4 percent alcohol. Evidence suggests that pulque may be as much as 4,000 years old and was drunk by the Aztecs. How pulque was sometimes consumed may have been similar to primitive wine and beer, with a lot of added ingredients. In fact, there are several recorded instances in the seventeenth century where Spaniards chastised the Native Americans for mixing pulque with herbs, spices, and fruit. One particular Aztec beverage, tepache, includes the rinds of pineapple and spices. More evidence of early mixologists at work! There are even early indications that, despite the Aztecs' strictures against drunkenness, pulque was consumed with great enthusiasm (and sometimes ill effects). One temple site in Mexico shows a pictograph of an overly enthusiastic drinker evacuating his bowels.

The one thing we're missing here is spirits. You can certainly make beer-tails and wine-tails—and pulque-tails if you will—and we'll see they had their place in early colonial America before the birth of the cocktail. But when we think mixed drinks, we think of vodka, gin, and Bourbon. So where do spirits come from then, and when did they arrive on the scene?

THE INVENTION OF SPIRITS

There are indications of distillation in ancient Greece, but disappointingly, the liquid in question was water. Aristotle wrote about the desalination of sea water more than 3,000 years ago in his treatise *Meteorologica*: "Salt water, when it turns into vapor, becomes sweet and the vapor does not form salt water when it condenses again." Great for making water potable, though it was not yet applied to alcohol, the "water of life," or "aqua vitae." Because distillation is not solely about spirits, the technology appears in bits and pieces throughout the ancient world. The distillation of alcohol doesn't begin until the first century in what is now modern-day Pakistan. And in the eighth century during the Islamic Golden Age, Persian alchemist Jābir ibn Hayyān (known in Europe as Geber) developed an alembic still that could produce spirits. That design would be the basis for modern stills—and even the word "alcohol" itself comes to us from Arabic. By understanding the technology of distillation, we can better see how this practice makes its way into the Americas.

The most basic aspect of distillation is that water and alcohol boil at different temperatures, 212°F and 173.1°F, respectively. That means when you boil alcohol such as a fruit wine or grain-based beer (the "mash" or "wort" as it is called), the vapor that boils off first is the alcohol. If one engineers an apparatus like a tube or an arm or neck, it's possible to capture a more concentrated amount of alcohol that follows the steam through condensation. There are primitive ways of doing this and then new, more modern ways, such as a column that allows for continuous distillation, patented by Irishman Aeneas Coffey in 1830 and responsible for most of America's bourbon and whiskey. Either way, ethanol contains some poisonous and some undesirable flavor compounds that need to be separated from the spirit intended to be drunk. Those portions are called the heads and the tails, and are at the beginning (heads) or end (tails) of the still's run. The middle portion, or the drinkable part, is referred to as the heart.

SPIRITS IN MESOAMERICA

A few months after the seminar we held at Tales of the Cocktail, David Suro-Piñera hosted Drs. McGovern and Healan along with a group of bartenders, including me, on a trip to western Jalisco in Mexico. In that region, some evidence exists that there was distillation well before the arrival of Columbus—possibly as early as the first century CE. The evidence exists near Colima, where archaeologists found a simple, two-chambered clay pot at a funerary site dating back to the Capacha period in Mexico around the first century (thus named a Capacha pot). The theory is, if it was heated from beneath with fire and sealed on top with a dish that collects the steam along its bottom, out would slowly drip a shimmery, potent liquid into a small cup suspended by strings. They re-created the pot and actually distilled using it.

But that they could doesn't mean they did. This pot could be used for distillation, but there is no clear evidence that it was. Also, the smaller cup used to capture the liquid was never found. Dr. McGovern took a few small shards to analyze for organic material that might relate to the production of a distillate. That is done by first finding a biomarker, or organic compound that can be linked to an agave spirit. So we also visited traditional mezcal (and raicilla, another traditional name for agave spirits) production sites. Once a biomarker is established, then you crush the shards and put them under mass spectrometry to determine the organic material and search for the match.

Unfortunately, we don't know the full results yet. However, it raises a compelling possibility. Maybe distillation was practiced in the Americas before anywhere else. So while we know that the cocktail was invented in America, about 300 years after the arrival of Columbus, maybe the first spirits were made here too, nearly 1,500 years before that.

CHAPTER ONE

Fish House Punch
p36

OUR FOUNDING DRINKERS

1490s > 1790s

While we've seen that alcoholic mixed drinks existed in North America before Columbus, his arrival in the New World changed the game. It opened the floodgates to centuries of immigration, commerce, and conquest, creating a veritable cocktail of people and cultures that would ultimately give birth to, well, the cocktail itself.

To understand how the cocktail became the quintessential American drink, you have to look at how its basic ingredients came to the continent, and the people who brought them here. You might call them our Founding Drinkers. No matter what their region of origin, they almost always brought their favorite drink with them—or tried their best to re-create it here. But the different geography, climate, and available ingredients forced them to develop new drinking habits, too. Their creativity and ingenuity in finding ways to get soused in this land knew no bounds. By exploring the ingredients that would fill early Americans' tankards, mugs, and punch bowls, we get a peek into what eventually would fill their cocktail glasses.

SPANISH SHERRY, THE DRINK OF PIRATES

Most Americans today don't think much about sherry. And when they do, they associate it with the sweet cream sherry sipped by their grandparents and great-grandparents. But traditional Spanish sherry is delicious and was a common mixer in America's cocktail golden age of the nineteenth century. It was even the star of its own wildly popular drink called the Sherry Cobbler, a refreshing mix of sherry, sugar, and citrus, shaken and poured over crushed ice. It was so famous—and so strongly associated with this country—that Charles Dickens even mentioned it in his satire about America, *The Life and Adventures of Martin Chuzzlewit*. Only recently has sherry been rediscovered by a new generation of mixologists. (I even opened a sherry bar in my hometown of Washington, D.C., to help introduce this neglected fortified wine to modern drinkers.) But sherry has a connection with American drinking that's much older than the Greatest Generation.

The first European drink likely to have landed in the so-called "New World" was Spanish sherry, brought over by Christopher Columbus himself. It was one of the provisions loaded onto his ships at the ports of Palos de la Frontera, Cádiz, and Sanlúcar, before sailing to what he thought were the East Indies. These cities were the launching point of Spanish exploration and treasure ships—and they also happened to be great producers of sherry.

About a century later, sherry would be in the holds and on the lips of notorious pirates and privateers before rum made its debut in the West Indies. The most famous sherry swiller was English "sea dog" Sir Francis Drake. Drake was the first Englishman to circumnavigate the globe, which he accomplished while plundering Spanish settlements along the way under the auspices of Queen Elizabeth I. As Spanish King Philip II began building his dreaded armada to invade England, Drake made a preemptive strike in 1587, raiding the ships harbored in the city of Cádiz. He destroyed enough of Spain's ships to delay the attempted invasion of England by a year. But more important for our story, he also carried away nearly 3,000 barrels of Spanish sherry. Londoners developed a great taste for the stolen stuff, which they called Sack, and would pass on this predilection to the people who would go on to settle Virginia and the other English colonies.

THAT FAMILIAR ENGLISH PINT

In the same year that Drake was popularizing Spanish sherry in London, his fellow Englishman John White led a voyage of more than one hundred men, women, and children to the colony at Roanoke off the coast of North Carolina. White had been there once before. He and his fellow settlers were actually rescued by Drake and dropped off back in England after relations with Native American tribes went sour and supplies got scarce. But published accounts of that first settlement described the bountiful foods and natural wonders that would await their countrymen, if they would just make the voyage across the Atlantic to this new land they called Virginia.

One thing an Englishman couldn't do without, however, was a good pint. And while there wasn't any barley handy in America, there was native corn everywhere. Writing in 1588 in what would be the first promotional brochure to entice colonists to move to Virginia, explorer Thomas Hariot assured his readers that they wouldn't have to give up their favorite drink.

He described a malt they had created from corn, "whereof was brewed as good ale as was to be desired. It also could be used, with the addition of hops, to produce a good beer."

Beer was actually important to the colonists' survival because the English were notoriously suspicious of water, which they considered to be hazardous to human health. This was not entirely without merit, considering the unsanitary conditions in crowded cities like London. They saw beer as a healthy alternative for breakfast, lunch, and dinner. When the new Roanoke settlement started to run low on provisions, it sent White back to London for help. He got waylaid by the newly rebuilt Spanish Armada, and didn't make it back to America for three more years. By then, the Roanoke colony had disappeared without a trace, and so had its corn ale. When the English made their next attempt at settlement in 1607 in Jamestown, they put help-wanted ads in London newspapers to entice experienced brewers to settle there.

Beer—or rather the lack of it—also played a large role in America's most famous origin story: the Pilgrims and the *Mayflower*. The ship's intended destination was the mouth of the Hudson River, but when it made landfall in Cape Cod, the captain determined the beer supply wouldn't sustain his crew for the ride home to England. Thus the Pilgrims landed at Plymouth Rock—or, more accurately, were pushed out by the captain. One of the first structures they built in their new home besides a church was a brew house, and a tavern was not far behind. The Puritans, those even more religious English settlers who arrived later in 1630 on the Arbella, were carrying almost three times more booze than water, including beer, cider, wine, and spirits. They were anything but puritanical when it came to the judicious use of wine and beer. In a famous 1673 sermon called "Wo to Drunkards," Boston pastor (and later president of Harvard) Increase Mather described these drinks as a "good creature of God."

To satisfy their cravings for beer, our forebears had to get creative with their ingredients. As this seventeenth-century verse suggests, these early Americans showed the same kind of ingenuity that would later characterize modern-day American craft brewers: "If Barley be wanting to make into malt / We must be content and think it no fault; / For we can make liquor to sweeten our lips / Of pumpkins and parsnips and walnut tree chips."

Persimmons and spruce were other favorite ingredients, but Americans eventually got the hang of making their own malt the traditional way. And it was often our Founding Mothers who were doing the early brewing: women were typically in charge of making the household's beer, and became extremely skilled brewers. Beer in America soon became plentiful, and was an integral part of the family table for men, women, and children.

But some were already worrying about just *how much* early Americans were taking refuge in their cups. In his "Wo to Drunkards" sermon, Increase Mather cautioned his fellow Puritans about the dangers of over-imbibing and to not drink "a Cup of Wine more than is good for him." The seeds of temperance, one of America's most effective social movements and the bane of drinkers, were already being planted.

THE ELUSIVE GRAPE

Early colonists not only tried to reproduce their favorite beer but turned their skills to wine as well. Reports back from Roanoke in 1584 described the land as "so full of grapes … that I think in all the world the like abundance is not to be found." The first American wines were likely created from those grapes by French or Spanish settlers in modern-day Florida and South Carolina in the 1560s. European colonizers saw North America as one extended vineyard ripe for wine production.

The colony of Jamestown even advertised for experienced winemakers. The Virginia Company in London sent some from the Languedoc region of France in 1619, and even passed a law that year requiring all households to plant and tend vines for winemaking. King James I hoped to replace the vice of Virginian tobacco (he famously wrote his own anti-smoking screed) with the virtue of wine as the colony's chief industry. The Frenchmen, though, realized they could make more money growing tobacco, and that most American grapes did not produce good wine. The more extreme climate shifts between sweltering summers and early frosts were partly to blame, as were mold and pests like the phylloxera, an American-born mite that would later wreak havoc on Old World vines. Luckily seventeenth-century foodie Sir Kenelm Digby developed the modern wine bottle in England—which was more durable and prevented sunlight from spoiling its contents—allowing American colonists to enjoy wine from Europe.

A century later, the Founding Fathers became passionate about trying to again jumpstart a native wine industry to wean them off expensive European imports. Benjamin Franklin's *Poor Richard's Almanack* in 1743 provided a do-it-yourself guide on how to make wine from backwoods grapes, claiming it could produce a "wholesome sprightly Claret ... not inferior to that which passeth for French claret." Perhaps it's telling that Franklin would later spend a decade as our minister to France, where he could more readily quaff the real deal in Paris. His successor in that role, Thomas Jefferson, was considered America's first wine connoisseur. Jefferson traveled throughout Burgundy and Bordeaux taking copious notes and sampling the foreign goods, then later experimented with European vines at his mountaintop home, Monticello.

Jefferson, Franklin, and other Founding Fathers helped encourage a Tuscan winemaker named Filippo Mazzei to come to America and plant vineyards to rival Europe's. Jefferson convinced him to set up a wine company on land neighboring Monticello, but Mazzei's European vines were soon dispatched by a spring frost. The Revolutionary War permanently derailed the short-lived experiment as this Italian immigrant winemaker joined the patriotic cause—a boon for American liberty, but a loss for American wine. (Happily, Mazzei's land would once again become a lovely vineyard more than 200 years later, called Jefferson Vineyards.)

Meanwhile, the Spanish were having better luck, producing wine and brandy as a sacrament (and a refresher) for their missions in modern-day Texas, New Mexico, and California. Phylloxera hadn't made it to the West, and the Spanish grape they chose, later known as the Mission grape, did well in those hot, dry climates. On the East Coast, it would take another century or two for a native industry to take root. In the meantime, it was imported wine from France, Italy, Portugal, and the Spanish Canary Islands that filled the cellars of early America's elites. The most popular were wines from the Portuguese archipelago of Madeira. Ships bound for America stopped there last to fill their holds with supplies, which often included casks of Madeira wine. To help preserve them for the long sea voyage, wine makers developed the custom of fortifying their wines with neutral spirits, which prevented them from turning sour. Drinkers in those faraway ports would soon discover that it was the sea voyage itself that made this fortified wine taste so good. The hot conditions in the ship holds and the constant jostling gave Madeira its distinctive taste. Not only did the wine survive and improve during long sea voyages, it was also cheaper because of a favored trade deal between England and Portugal. Thus Madeira would become the favorite drink of well-to-do American colonists, including just about all the Founding Fathers. George Washington was said to finish his nightly dinner with three glasses of the stuff.

FRUIT BRANDY, THE ORIGINAL AMERICAN SPIRIT

You can't have a cocktail without a spirit. But in the early days of colonization, Americans had no native spirit to speak of. If they were wealthy, colonists were importing European wines. The rest of us were getting by brewing beer or hard cider. It was cider, though, that produced the colonies' first widely distilled spirits—fruit brandies. While the grapes of the Old World had trouble adapting, apples, pears, and peaches were doing just fine. The Pilgrims brought apple seeds with them, and planted the first apple trees this side of the Atlantic. Farther south, peaches were planted by the Spanish during their early explorations.

Most fruit orchards in farmers' backyards were not for eating, though. They were more valuable for making alcoholic cider. Many of these early apple varieties were not that tasty, but they made delicious cider, which started to replace beer at the American table in the 1700s. Long before he became president, John Adams was one of the many early Americans to start the day by imbibing hard cider for breakfast. And it was relatively easy to turn hard cider into hard liquor. Farmers simply left it outside to freeze in the winter months. Removing the frozen water left the alcohol behind, thereby jacking up its potency and producing what became known as applejack.

In the early 1700s, Scottish immigrant William Laird used his distilling skills to make applejack and distilled apple brandy from the plentiful orchards of New Jersey (there's a reason it became known as the Garden State). The drink was so ubiquitous in the region that it was called "Jersey Lightning." The Laird family became well known for producing a fine "cyder spirit," with George Washington requesting the family recipe sometime around 1760, so that he could produce his own at Mount Vernon. Laird & Co. was founded in 1780, and is the country's oldest licensed distillery, continuing to produce applejack and apple brandy (now made from Virginia apples, not far from Jefferson's home of Monticello) to the delight of modern mixologists.

Even more prized in the South was good peach brandy. As Italian nobleman Luigi Castiglioni described it in his book *Travels in the United States of North America* in the late 1780s, "the difficulty and expense of obtaining rum and other liquors in regions far from the sea induced the Virginians to make their own brandy from peaches." The result could be extremely tasty and packed a punch. As Castiglioni said, "The liquor is very strong and has a pleasing and delicate fragrance."

Now in the modern-day bar, peach-flavored anything gets a bad rap because of two words: peach schnapps. There's an unspoken bartender rule that if a customer orders a Sex on the Beach, a Fuzzy Navel, or any drink with peach schnapps, regardless of the person's perceived age, they get carded. As we'll see later, peach schnapps was a product of the dark days of the American cocktail, first becoming popular in the 1970s. Back in the 1770s, George Washington never made or had Sex on the Beach as far as I know, but he did make a fine peach brandy, and even gave it away as prized gifts to diplomats and luminaries like the Marquis de Lafayette. Cocktail historian Dave Wondrich calls peach brandy the original American spirit, a drink that wouldn't have been imbibed back home in Europe. Good, aged peach brandy became prized by wealthy Americans in the late 1700s, and was the ultimate gentleman's drink.

Castiglioni said the habit was to drink this as one would drink brandy or rum—with a little water—or mix it "with sugar or syrup like maraschino" made from plentiful cherries. Now that's starting to sound like a cocktail. Because of its milder taste, peach brandy was a particularly good blender for mixed drinks and punches, early precursors to the cocktail. One of the most famous drinks in early America, Fish House Punch, featured peach brandy.

This iconic punch had its origins in Philadelphia. In 1732, more than forty years before we would declare ourselves independent of Great Britain, a collection of Philadelphian citizens declared their own, fictional mini-state. They called it the Colony in Schuylkill, after reportedly making a treaty with the local Native American tribes. It was an angler's club for upper-class Philadelphians who liked to fish, and its primary activities seemed to be eating, fishing, and drinking like fish. The Fish House in question was a clubhouse built on the Schuylkill River. Like most other gentlemen social clubs at the time, it developed its own distinctive punch, combining peach brandy, French Cognac, and rum. The group still exists today as the Schuylkill Fishing Company, and is considered America's oldest continuous dining club. And they still serve Fish House Punch.

Eventually, peach brandy would be dethroned by cheap rum and then whiskey, and all but forgotten by American drinkers. Only recently has it been rediscovered by intrepid distillers and mixologists, who are once again giving us a taste of this early American spirit.

RAMBUNCTIOUS RUM AND RUINOUS GIN

Even before there was peach brandy, a new spirit came onto the scene in the mid-1600s that would change the way Americans drank, and get us even closer to the cocktail. It had all the qualities Americans wanted in their tipple. It was strong, it was relatively easy to make, and it was cheap. It was best mixed with some water, sugar, and citrus. It was called rum.

As with sherry, the origins of rum in America can also be traced back to Columbus. Before his career as an explorer, Columbus was a sugar merchant on the island of Madeira, which was known back then more for sugar than its wine. Recognizing a good climate when he saw one, he packed sugarcane in his ships' holds for his second voyage across the Atlantic. Within a hundred years, the sugarcane he introduced to the island of Hispaniola (modern-day Haiti and Dominican Republic) would dominate the entire Caribbean economy. It would also unleash two major forces that would shape American society: slavery and rum.

Sugar production relied on brutal slave labor, first from indigenous peoples and then from enslaved Africans forcibly brought to the Caribbean. An unintended byproduct was molasses, a sweet-smelling, sticky substance that was initially viewed as an industrial waste product and often dumped into the ocean. Eventually someone in the Caribbean (likely in Barbados) discovered that molasses could be turned into rum. By the 1700s, a flood of rum and molasses would emanate from the sugar-producing Caribbean colonies of the English, French, and Dutch. They used enslaved Africans to plant and harvest the sugar, and either made rum on-site from the resulting molasses, or sold the molasses to the English North American colonies to be made into rum at small distilleries up and down the Eastern Seaboard. Early Americans would just as likely associate rum with Boston as with Barbados—although the good stuff came from the islands.

Rum soon replaced sherry and Spanish wines as the booze and booty of pirates who preyed on the ships carrying it between the Caribbean and the Atlantic. It also began to supplant the beer, wine, cider, and fruit brandy drunk by colonists. It became a part of everyday life, particularly for the common folk, and was used as both currency and cure-all. But clergy and public officials warned about the health effects of a drink so cheap, plentiful, and potent. James Edward Oglethorpe, the idealistic founder of Georgia, tried to ban rum in his new colony, fearing it would corrupt his utopian experiment. (That didn't last long.) Already known as Kill Devil perhaps because of its potency, it was also decried as Demon Rum from the pulpits because of the widespread drunkenness it caused. Puritan minister Cotton Mather, the zealous son of Increase Mather, worried in a 1708 sermon that a flood of rum would "Overwhelm all good Order among us."

Meanwhile, back in the Mother Country, authorities were also wringing their hands about widespread drunkenness. But there the culprit was gin. It was first imported from Holland, where it was called *genever*, based on the Dutch word for juniper, one of its principal ingredients. It was also known as "Dutch Courage" because of the alcohol-induced bravery it inspired in soldiers. In English cities, it became known as "Mother's Ruin," because it was strong, cheap, and easier to make than rum. Soon gin was consumed by—and was consuming—a wide swathe of the urban population. It was called the Gin Craze, and Parliament would try to tax and regulate gin throughout the 1700s to curb its abuse. The panic eventually fizzled out, but because of gin's bad reputation back home and the dominance of rum in the colonies, it wouldn't become a staple of American drinking until the 1800s.

Despite a growing backlash against rum, it was considered the modern drink of the New World up until the American Revolution. In his book *And a Bottle of Rum: A History of the New World in Ten Cocktails*, writer and historian Wayne Curtis describes how it represented independence from the Old World's drinking habits and something new under the sun. It would even spark a revolution and the birth of a spirited new republic, in many ways built on rum.

THE TAVERN: A PLACE TO MIX (DRINKS)

By the 1700s, Americans had most of the basic ingredients they needed to start mixing drinks. They also had countless taverns in which to do their imbibing. In this new country, taverns weren't just watering holes. They served as hotels, post offices, public meeting spaces, and courthouses. They were so important to public life that the Puritans mandated that every town have them, and even fined the ones that didn't. They were a place where both men and women gathered, and many women actually owned or ran their own taverns, despite the limited legal rights they had at the time.

Some taverns were rowdy, and others were more like social clubs for the elite, complete with access to a library and newspapers. But they all became a place to unwind over spirited conversation and spirited libations. Though in many, the alcoholic fare was probably unremarkable. One traveling Englishman, a British prisoner of war during the Revolution who still seemed to have the run of the countryside, complained that all he could get in the rural taverns or ordinaries of Virginia was "peach brandy and whiskey," neither being to his taste. But American tavern keepers in more populated areas began to compete for business by offering up ever more creative mixed drinks. Most used peach brandy or rum as a base, adding ingredients like water, sugar, beer, cider, lime juice, mint, nutmeg, and clove. Vinegar-based fruit shrubs were also used as a mixer, particularly when more exotic fresh citrus was lacking. (Those too have made a comeback behind the bar.)

Mimbos, Bombos, Whistle Bellys, Rattleskulls, Sangarees, Syllabubs, and Toddys were just some of the colorfully named concoctions common at local taverns. The Flip was an extremely popular mix of beer and rum, and called for the use of a heated iron loggerhead, a kind of poker called a flip-dog, to put into the concoction to create its foamy head. (When the poker wasn't being heated in the fire to create a Flip, it was sometimes used as a drunken weapon, hence the phrase "to be at loggerheads.") The Julep, a favorite "medicinal" drink among early Virginians, first combined rum, water, and sugar, often taken at breakfast. It would eventually take the country by storm, and be popularized with mint, brandy or bourbon, and ice. But more and more, rum punch became the drink of choice for colonists.

As with the birth of the cocktail, punch's origin story is murky. David Wondrich has traced its beginnings to British sailors in the seventeenth century, who brought back exotic new ingredients found in India and Indonesia. It began as sailors' grog, that ration of rum diluted with water and seasoned with sugar, lemons, or lime to lessen the bite. Sailors brought punch back to their home ports in England, where it spread among the common classes and elites alike. It became *the* way to consume spirits, from lowly taverns to aristocratic clubhouses and homes. And the punch bowl itself became a ubiquitous vessel.

Punch was uniquely suited to the American colonies. With scattered settlements, it was an easy way to serve travelers and locals alike. It was a communal—one might say democratic—experience, with citizens partaking from the same bowl, debating the issues of the day, and sharing news. Consider it a shared version of a cocktail. And it was in those very taverns over punch bowls that the American spirit was forged. Because soon the colonists and the Mother Country would be at loggerheads, and the ingredients in punch would be directly tied to revolution.

A REVOLUTION … IN DRINKING

Throughout the 1700s, Parliament tried to raise revenue from its American colonies by taxing what they drank. Tea may spring first to mind, but the original target was rum. The Molasses Act of 1733 taxed molasses, sugar, and rum, trying to force New England merchants to buy from fellow British colonies in the Caribbean rather than their preferred French Caribbean vendors. American merchants basically ignored the act and became adept at smuggling, 200 years before the rum-running between the islands and the mainland that became common during Prohibition.

In 1764, Parliament passed the Sugar Act, which was also the first time that duties were placed on the beloved Madeira and other wines from Portugal. That was followed by the Stamp Act and the Townshend Acts that placed taxes on all types of different products, including tea. Soon revolution was being hatched over rum-fortified punch in American taverns like the Green Dragon in Boston, where the Sons of Liberty met to plot the Boston Tea Party. More than any other place, it was the taverns that became the communication centers among the colonies. Historian Christine Sismondo, author of *America Walks into a Bar: A Spirited History of Taverns and Saloons, Speakeasies and Grog Shops*, called them the "telegraph line of the era." In Philadelphia, while the newly formed Continental Congress met in Carpenters' Hall to plan a response to the British, the real business of revolution happened at the refined City Tavern nearby over drinks.

As the American colonies went to war with England, General George Washington knew that alcohol was also crucial for military success. "The benefits arising from the moderate use of strong Liquor have been experienced in All Armies, and are not to be disputed," he wrote from camp to John Hancock in 1777. How else would troops make it through that Valley Forge winter without peach brandy, applejack, or rum to warm them? In his General Orders from March 1, 1778, written during a snowstorm at Valley Forge, Washington praised the "uncomplaining Patience" of his troops despite the scanty provisions, displaying "the spirit of soldiers." But he also made sure those soldiers had spirits, ordering a ration of a gill of rum or whiskey for each man.

Looking back nearly fifty years later in 1818, former revolutionary and second U.S. president John Adams famously summed up the tie between rum and revolution in a letter to his friend, William Tudor, Sr.: "I know not why We Should blush to confess that Molasses was an essential Ingredient in American independence. Many great Events have proceeded from much Smaller Causes." (We'll see in the next chapter that right about that time, Tudor's son Frederic was revolutionizing American drinking on his own by introducing what would become an essential ingredient—ice.)

While the Revolutionary War was in part tied to Americans' love of rum, it also sealed rum's fate. The disruption of the molasses trade during the war caused Americans to turn to another spirit made from more readily available ingredients: the upstart whiskey. It was created from the boundless fields of rye and corn, and produced by the Scotch-Irish immigrants who brought their distilling and drinking habits with them to the mountains of Pennsylvania, Maryland, Virginia, and the new territories of Kentucky and Tennessee. Its homegrown ingredients that didn't depend on trading with Britain or France gave whiskey the boost it needed. Drinking whiskey would become a sign of patriotism in the new United States of America.

OUR FUZL'D FOUNDING DRINKERS

Throughout our early history, the Founding Fathers and Mothers were both observers of America's peculiar drinking habits and willing participants. In 1737, Benjamin Franklin published *The Drinkers Dictionary*, a list of over two hundred ways of describing how to get drunk. It's considered one of the first collections of uniquely American colloquialisms (helpfully alphabetized), "gather'd wholly from the modern Tavern-Conversation of Tiplers." Some are familiar to the modern ear, like "Boozy," "Intoxicated," "Tipsey," and "In his Cups." Some suggest what Americans were getting drunk on, like "Been at Barbadoes" (for drinking too much rum). Others are more mysterious, like "Wamble Crop'd," "Fuzl'd," "Nimptopsical," and "Pungey," but you get the general drift.

Politicians also tried guiding Americans' drinking habits from the top. Leaders like Thomas Jefferson and Alexander Hamilton often spoke out against the ubiquitous rum and newly popular whiskey they saw as corrupting the American work ethic and spirit—one of the few things they agreed on. By the time George Washington became president, the average American was consuming 5.8 gallons of pure alcohol a year. Within a few decades, that peaked at 7.1 gallons, as Americans overtook their European counterparts as the world's biggest drinkers. (For comparison, modern Americans drink about 2.3 gallons of pure alcohol each year.) Our ancestors were certainly imbibing a lot of booze with their newfound democracy.

Dr. Benjamin Rush, a physician and signer of the Declaration of Independence, began to campaign against hard liquors, which helped lay the groundwork for the Temperance movement. For the average American, he created a handy "Physical and Moral Thermometer" to show the benefit of Temperance and the slippery slope to Intemperance. On the Temperance side, water had long since shed its bad reputation, and was enshrined alongside milk as the best thing for "Serenity of Mind, Reputation, Long Life & Happiness." But so was "small beer," which averaged about 3 percent alcohol, and was a common drink on the family table. Cider, wine, and strong beer were also okay to throw back, because they contributed to "Cheerfulness, Strength and Nourishment." Like in early colonial days, these drinks were still considered part of a healthy diet for adults and children in moderation. But when you crossed over into punch, you were starting to imbibe dangerously. You were inviting "Idleness" and "Peevishness," and could end up suffering the effects of "Puking" or "Tremors." What college student hasn't been there?

It only went down on his thermometer as you moved into toddys, grog, flips, and shrubs. Next on the list was the closest thing we've seen to the cocktail, although in a reverse ratio and not yet known by that name: "Bitters infused with spirits." All those spirits were equally suspect, including usquebaugh (whiskey), rum, gin, and brandy, particularly when imbibed morning, day, and night. That was liable to lead to swindling, perjury, burglary, murder, suicide (in that order), and a trip to the "Poor-house" or the "Gallows." Others thought the fumes from hard alcohol could lead to spontaneous combustion while walking down the street.

Rush was a respected voice around the country, and had been Surgeon General of the Continental Army. His theories about alcohol addiction were ahead of their time, but expressed a worry that many of the Founding Fathers shared—that the new nation's promise was being ruined by drink. He and his friend Jefferson tried to steer their fellow Americans away from hard spirits and towards wine, with Jefferson noting from his perch as American ambassador in Paris that cheap wine was the only "antidote to the bain of whiskey." (He, of course, only drank the expensive kind.)

But Americans had minds of their own when it came to drinking, and at this point refused to be scared sober by elite opinion. That's because our Founding Drinkers were not necessarily our Founding Fathers. They were all of us: every man and woman (and child) making do with what was available, and adding their own creative spin. It was the average American that helped turn a variety of global influences and ingredients into something that would be considered uniquely American the world over. And that would be called the cocktail.

FISH HOUSE PUNCH

Thankfully, fish has nothing to do with this tasty punch imbibed by practically all of our American worthies, including George Washington and the Marquis de Lafayette. Good old peach brandy is the star of this drink, but rum and Cognac hold their own. The recipe was passed down by generations of members of the Schuylkill Fishing Company, which claims to be the oldest uninterrupted social club in the English-speaking world. The ingredients made their way into print in 1862, thanks to America's first superstar bartender, Jerry Thomas. While the recipe has changed throughout the years, cocktail historian David Wondrich provides this modern approximation to the original.

PUNCH BOWL (8-12 QTS)

Peels of 8 lemons, plus 16 ounces fresh lemon juice
2 ½ cups Demerara sugar
16 ounces boiling water
1 (750-milliliter) bottle Smith & Cross Traditional Jamaican Rum (or other strong, pungent Jamaican rum)
12 ounces VSOP Cognac
12 ounces real peach brandy (not peach-flavored brandy)
3 quarts (96 ounces) cold water
Whole nutmeg, grated, and lemon wheels for garnish

Muddle lemon peels with sugar in the bottom of a punch bowl until a thick paste forms (that is called the oleo saccharum). Add boiling water. Allow to cool, then remove peels and add lemon juice and spirits. Add cold water quart by quart to taste. Grate nutmeg on top and garnish with lemon wheels. *Makes 25 servings.*

SYLLABUB

The Syllabub is a drink that is as much dessert as beverage. Though I agree with Hemingway's purported declaration, "Any man who eats dessert is not drinking enough," the Syllabub begs the question: Why choose? The drink's oddest part, besides its name, is how it spawned so many objects to produce it, from glassware with spouts to machines powered by bellows to whip the froth. I'm a fan of a good gadget, so I would keep it around for that reason alone. But it's also delicious.

SMALL GLASS WITH FLUTED TOP (5½-7½ OUNCES; WE USE A BEER SAMPLING GLASS.)

Drink:
16 ounces Madeira, medium (e.g., Bual or Verdelho)
16 ounces dry Riesling
8 ounces confectioners sugar
6 ounces fresh lemon juice
¾ cup fresh pineapple, chopped
zest of 2 lemons
2 rosemary sprigs

Whipped cream:
4 ounces Madeira, medium
4 ounces dry Riesling
2 ounces confectioners sugar
1 ½ ounces fresh lemon juice
¼ cup fresh pineapple, chopped
zest of half a lemon
1 rosemary sprig
10 ounces heavy cream

Combine drink ingredients, seal in a container, and refrigerate overnight. In a separate container, combine whipped cream ingredients, seal, and refrigerate overnight. Strain and discard solids from cream mixture with a fine mesh sieve, then whip into a thick lather, until stiff peaks form. Seal and refrigerate overnight. To serve, strain and discard solids from the drink mixture then pour 4-ounce portions into each glass. Top with whipped cream. *Makes 10 Servings.*

APPLE TODDY

Toddys are a class of drink that predate the cocktail. Though we commonly think of them today as hot drinks, they can be served either hot or cold, depending on the season. An apple toddy is just one iteration, but in eighteenth-century America, apple toddys ruled, particularly in Maryland. Toddy-makers took great pride in their recipes and attention to detail, and they frequently aged their drinks anywhere from a few months to years at a time. In the late nineteenth century, they were aged during the stretch from Thanksgiving to Christmas. How they could wait weeks for this sweet, delicious beverage, I will never know.

TEA CUP (6 OZ.)

2 apples, roasted with cloves and a cinnamon stick, sliced (recipe below)
15 ounces apple brandy
15 ounces water
4 ounces confectioners sugar

To make the roasted apples: Pre-heat oven to 400°F. Peel and core apples, then stud 5 cloves into each apple, and place cinnamon stick in the center (where the core was removed) and place on a baking sheet. Roast on the center rack until golden (about 30-45 minutes, depending on size and ripeness*). When cooled, muddle slices of roasted apples into a glass with brandy, water, and sugar and macerate for at least one day. Strain off solids, then age for one month to a year in the refrigerator. When ready to serve, measure 4 ounces of liquid and pour into tea cup. (Can be served warm or chilled.) *Makes 1 drink.*

* If apples are lacking sweetness or unripe, dip in simple syrup (one part sugar to one part water) before roasting.

STONE FENCE

This mixed drink had a starring role in an early American victory during the Revolution. Ethan Allen and his Green Mountain Boys planned their daring raid on the British Fort Ticonderoga in 1775 at the Catamount Tavern in Old Bennington. Legend has it that they found courage in their cups by throwing back a drink called the Stone Fence, a pleasing and bracing mixture of hard cider and rum that was common at the time. The Green Mountain Boys successfully stormed the fort and seized it from a few surprised and sleepy British soldiers, bolstering the American cause. The drink started with rum, but rum was replaced with rye as it took its place as the king of American spirits (I featured the rye version at Southern Efficiency, my whiskey bar in D.C.). The origins of the name are not known for sure, but could refer to the feeling that resulted when imbibing too many—namely, running headlong through a country field into an impenetrable stone fence.

HIGHBALL OR COLLINS GLASS (8-10 OZ.)

2 ounces rye whiskey, rum, or brandy
Dash Angostura bitters
Apple cider
Mint sprig for garnish

Pour the spirit into highball or Collins glass, and then add a dash of bitters. Top with ice and fill glass to the brim with cider. Stir, garnish with mint, and serve. *Makes 1 drink.*

GENERAL'S ORDERS (ORIGINAL)

I created this drink as the official cocktail of the National Archives' Spirited Republic exhibit and lecture series, which was the genesis of this book. The drink is named after Washington's General Orders from Valley Forge on March 1, 1778, which issued a ration of spirits to his long-suffering troops. The modern cocktail combines the colonial standby spirit of rum with the upstart American spirit of rye whiskey, and a personal favorite of the general: cherry bounce, a cordial made with brandy, cherry, and spice popular during the time period. Washington brought a canteen of it (along with Madeira and Port) while traveling to inspect the new American lands west of the Allegheny Mountains after the Revolutionary War in 1784. We use Cherry Heering as an able substitute, but if you want to drink the way Washington did, use Martha's own recipe, available on Mount Vernon's website.

HIGHBALL GLASS (10-12 OZ.)

1 ounce aged rum
½ ounce rye whiskey
¾ ounce fresh lemon juice
½ ounce simple syrup
¼ ounce Cherry Heering or Cherry Bounce
Dash of Angostura bitters

Combine all ingredients in shaker. Shake and strain into highball glass over ice. Garnish with a miniature American flag (optional).
Makes 1 drink.

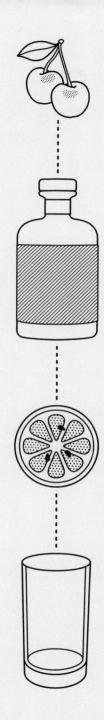

CHAPTER TWO

Old Fashioned
p60

BIRTH OF THE COCKTAIL

Since the earliest days of the Republic (and before), America has been a nation of drinks and drinkers. But in 1803, something happened that would later be seen as a milestone in the annals of American drinking. That year, President Thomas Jefferson doubled the size of the country with the Louisiana Purchase, bringing the bibulous city of New Orleans into the fold. As Meriwether Lewis and William Clark set off to explore this vast new tract of territory, counting wine and beer and whiskey rations as necessary provisions for their expedition to the Pacific, this simple line appeared in a humorous article in New Hampshire's *Farmer's Cabinet* newspaper: "Drank a glass of cocktail—excellent for the head … Call'd at the Doct's: found Burnham—he looked very wise—drank another glass of cocktail."

And thus the American cocktail was born, at least for cocktail historians. For while there are earlier mentions of the word coming out of London and Dublin, this is the first one anyone has found in America. Although it doesn't say what it is, we get a sense that it's medicinal in the loosest sense of the word, like those morning juleps Virginians so loved. Three years later, as Lewis and Clark were on their way back from the Oregon coast, their drinking rations having long dried up, the cocktail was helpfully defined for the first time in print. On May 13, 1806, Harry Croswell, editor of the Federalist newspaper *The Balance, and Columbian Repository* in Hudson, New York, decided to take a tally of a local candidate's gains and losses at the end of a recent political contest. Losses included the many drinks bought for would-be supporters, including rum grogs, brandy, gin slings, and bitters. Gains were listed as "Nothing." Despite the common practice of buying booze for votes, it seems as though it did little for this particular candidate, who ultimately lost his election.

But the news coverage did a lot for posterity, because under the losses category, the editor also listed "25 cock tails," in addition to the other drinks. This was a word that was apparently not known to all readers at the time. One curious subscriber wrote in, giving us a run-down of tippler's terminology that would have made Ben Franklin proud: "I have heard of a forum, of phlegm-cutter and fog driver, of wetting the whistle, of moistening the clay, of a fillip, a spur in the head, quenching a spark in the throat, of flip & c, but never in my life, though I have lived a good many years, did I hear of cock tail before."

Not to be stumped, Croswell responded: "As I make it a point, never to publish anything (under my editorial head) but which I can explain, I shall not hesitate to gratify the curiosity of my inquisitive correspondent: Cock tail, then is a stimulating liquor, composed of spirits of any kind, sugar, water, and bitters. ..." This followed with one final jab at his political rivals: "It is vulgarly called bittered sling, and is supposed to be an excellent electioneering potion, in as much as it renders the heart stout and bold, at the same time that it fuddles the head. It is said ... to be of great use to the democratic candidate: because, a person having swallowed a glass of it, is ready to swallow any thing else." A devout Federalist, Croswell had regularly published attacks against President Thomas Jefferson and his Democratic-Republicans, so much so that he was sued for seditious libel. (He was defended in a famous court case by none other than Federalist super-lawyer and future Broadway star Alexander Hamilton, just five months before his fateful duel.)

But incivility in politics was nothing new, nor was glad-handing over drinks. George Washington himself won his early elections by supplying voters with gallons of wine, beer, cider, rum, and punch. (He learned his lesson after losing his first election because he refused to treat voters with booze.) What was new was this unique American drink called the cocktail. It represented a break in drinking tradition from the communal punches and shared libations of the colonial period to a new republic dedicated to the pursuit of individual happiness. Within this very simple set of ingredients—spirits, sugar, water, and bitters—Americans could now customize and individualize their drinks to a large degree. And in the cocktail, the taste of the whole would certainly become greater than the sum of its parts, as Aristotle would say. But to see what that first cocktail would have tasted like, let's first examine each of these essential ingredients.

SPIRITS

The cocktail had versatility, in that just about any spirit could be used as a base. This set the stage for the countless variations of mixed drinks to come as new spirits and ingredients became available. But in early nineteenth-century America, the most common spirits would have been rum, brandy, gin, or increasingly, rye whiskey.

SUGAR

Refined sugar was commonly doled out in large loaves during this time period, rather than the small sugar cubes we see today. So it's probably better to think of this category more broadly as all class of sweeteners that were easily accessible to early Americans. Honey, molasses, syrup, and sorghum—all would have fit the bill. These gave body and sweetness to the drink, rounding off the harshness of the mostly unaged spirits that would have been used.

WATER

Today we associate cocktails with temperature: we want them cold. But in the early days, cocktails were served at room temperature. Rather than adding ice, which wouldn't have been a common practice until an American ice industry developed about mid-nineteenth century, bartenders mixed cocktails with a little water. (This was also the norm in mixed drinks before the cocktail. A traditional grog was rum mixed with water, another way to help soften the bite of substandard spirits.) Ice became the stand-in for water. As it's mixed in the drink, it also melts and dilutes it.

BITTERS

The above three ingredients are not what truly makes a cocktail; they were already commonly found in mixed drinks of the time. The transformative element was the addition of bitters, a compound tincture of citrus peels, spices, and botanicals. Bitters were commonly used as medicinal products to settle colonial stomachs, but they soon became the salt and pepper of the drinking world. In the nineteenth century, there were hundreds of varieties, each with their own unique taste. There were some truly famous standouts like Peychaud's and Angostura that are still staples today, while other popular brands like Boker's disappeared during Prohibition. The addition of bitters is the key to understanding what makes the cocktail unique. Without those essential dashes, your drink can taste flat. Bitters gives it a transformative flavoring that keeps you coming back for more.

But how do those ingredients come to be called a cocktail—especially since alternate names (like the vulgar "bittered sling") were floated? There's a lot to a name.

A COCKTAIL BY ANY OTHER NAME ...

Traveling to bars throughout the country, I think I've heard just about every possible cocktail creation myth, some with more frequency than others. In the French Quarter in New Orleans, tour guides will tell you that the first cocktail was a Sazerac. It's a beautiful cocktail, and certainly an American classic. It purportedly began as a combination of bitters and imported French brandy, later subbing in good old American rye whiskey shipped down the Mississippi. A Creole apothecary, Antoine Peychaud, would mix a version of it in small eggcups known in French as *coquetiers*. The Anglicized version in that polyglot city would end up being pronounced "cock-tails." Nice story, eh?

It has one fatal flaw though, according to cocktail historian and Washington, D.C. lawyer Phil Greene, who is also a Peychaud descendant. While doing genealogical research, he discovered that Antoine Peychaud was born in 1803, the same year that the word "cocktail" first appears in print in America, and three years before it was first defined. As Greene tells it, Antoine may have been a precocious lad, but mixing drinks while under the age of three? Still, Peychaud has an enduring legacy without being the inventor of the cocktail itself. He created Peychaud's Bitters, which are still an essential ingredient for cocktails today, including the famous Sazerac. Another story posits that tavern keepers pulled the dregs of near-empty barrels—early spirits were held in barrels and not bottles—mixed them together, and sold the concoctions at a discount. The spigot of a barrel was sometimes called a cock, and those dregs were known as the "tailings." Perhaps my favorite story though is about a Frenchman who plucked a feather from a rooster to stir his drink and called it a cocktail. Maybe this one is a tad too literal.

In an updated edition of his book *Imbibe!*, David Wondrich traced the origin story to another animal: the horse. Early bartenders and aristocratic drinkers often lived what was called the sporting life, betting on racehorses and billiards. Wondrich points to the habit of docking the tails of racehorses, which gave them the appearance of rooster tails. These horses were said to be a little more frisky, so "cock your tail up" became slang for a pick-me-up. "Cock-tail" was also a term for mixed breed racehorses, which could have been applied to these new forms of mixed drinks.

Another of Wondrich's findings point to the back end of a horse, and not its docked tail. He discovered an eighteenth-century reference in English papers to ginger being used as a stimulant to cock a horse's tail and make them peppier. The insertion point of the ginger was conveniently located just below the tail. This was a common practice apparently, and adopted as another slang term for a "picker upper." The evidence is there to point to this as the origin of the word, but not necessarily the drink.

There is really no concrete proof save a good tale to back up any of these origination myths. In the meantime, bartenders everywhere can still spin their own yarns from behind the bar and create their own origin stories. Whether their patrons will believe them is something altogether different, and depends on how much they've already swallowed on the other side of the bar. In the end though, all that mattered was the building blocks of these four ingredients, cocktail's DNA, if you will. This combination was pioneered in America, and Americans took this recipe and ran with it.

THE OLD FASHIONED

If you want to approximate what those early cocktails tasted like, well then, you need to fix yourself an Old Fashioned.

I'm not talking about the fruit cup that the Old Fashioned became, with pulverized cherries and oranges. I'm talking about the simple combination of rye whiskey, sugar, maybe a lemon or orange peel, and bitters, all stirred with ice. It's the one true drink formed of the cocktail's *prima materia*, conforming to the original definition from 1806. Though rye whiskey or bourbon is the spirit of choice for a standard Old Fashioned, you can use whatever base spirit you wish. It appears that many early Americans did just that with what they had available at the time. For example, in the early 1800s, there was a Gin Cocktail and a Brandy Cocktail. The Old Fashioned itself started life as the Whiskey Cocktail.

All of these cocktails followed the simple, four-ingredient recipe. A lemon or orange peel or other garnishes wouldn't be prevalent until later. If citrus was even available, it was considered "fancy" and an add-on. As cocktail culture—and indeed American culture—became more sophisticated, bartenders would start using more specialized sweet liqueurs like orange Curaçao, maraschino liqueur, absinthe, and vermouth, all coming from Europe. They started making so many versions of these "improved" cocktails, that some began arguing for a back-to-basics approach. Patrons demanded that simple, old-fashioned Whiskey Cocktail. And thus the Old Fashioned took its place as the grandfather of all cocktails, and the closest we can come today to tasting that original cocktail of our forebears.

A WHISKEY REVOLUTION

The whiskey that was an integral part of the Old Fashioned cocktail became the king of American spirits in the 1800s. The rum that was so popular during colonial days became too associated with the past for people eager to turn the page and write their own political (and drinking) history. In fact, the history of American whiskey stretches back even further, to the founding of the Virginia colony. English colonist George Thorpe came to the early settlement of Henricus in Virginia, just up the James River from Jamestown, to start a university and convert the Native Americans to Christianity. Along the way, historians believe he discovered a technique to distill beer made from the plentiful native corn to produce a whiskey that predated Kentucky bourbon by more than a century. Sadly, his technique was lost to history after the Powhatan Uprising in 1622—led by Chief Powhatan's younger brother Opechancanough, uncle to Pocahontas—which destroyed many of the settlements that had sprouted up along the James River. George Thorpe was killed, and his whiskey still would never be found. But Virginians today consider the Old Dominion the birthplace of this quintessential American spirit.

A hundred years later, waves of Scotch-Irish immigrants would pick up where Thorpe left off. They first came as indentured servants, but were soon actively recruited to the new colonies as a hardscrabble buffer in the western territories to the Native Americans who were increasingly being displaced. According to bourbon chronicler Dane Huckelbridge, nearly a quarter of a million Scotch-Irish emigrated to America before the Declaration of Independence, and most of them settled in the western parts of Pennsylvania, Maryland, and Virginia. They brought with them their techniques of distilling that had become entrenched in Ireland and Scotland. Their drink of choice was *uisce beatha*, the Gaelic name for "aqua vitae," which brought us the word "whiskey." They first made their American whiskey out of rye, the grain they were used to in the Old World, and that grew exceedingly well in the hills of Pennsylvania and Maryland.

After Americans won the Revolutionary War, they were also no longer prevented from streaming over the Appalachian Mountains by the English Crown, which had tried to honor treaties with Native Americans to keep those lands off limits to colonists. The fertile areas that would soon become the states of Kentucky and Tennessee were suddenly swarming with settlers, and would become major sources of whiskey production. Whiskey was the perfect drink of the American frontier. It was often made and consumed close to home, and it was also much easier to transport barrels of rye liquor to market than large bushels of the grain itself. But its ascendancy was almost thwarted early in George Washington's administration.

In fact, the first tax ever imposed by the new federal government was one imposed on distilled spirits. It was part of Federalist Alexander Hamilton's plan to help pay down America's debts after the war, but there was also a little social engineering under way. The Eastern elite already worried about how much ardent spirits the average American was drinking, and how it might threaten the economic and social order. The tax targeted all distilled spirits, but it hit whiskey the hardest. And the burden of paying it fell particularly on poorer, smaller farmers. Larger distillers, including George Washington himself, who operated the largest distillery in the nation at Mount Vernon, were able to pay a lower rate per gallon.

Opposition to the tax soon became widespread in the western part of many of the Southern states and came to a head in western Pennsylvania with the Whiskey Rebellion in 1794. Of course there was great irony in that the United States owed its existence, in part, to rebelling against taxes on what its citizens drank. Recognizing this, the new federal government wasted no time in quashing the uprising, with Distiller-in-Chief Washington mounting his horse and actually leading the charge.

While the conflict itself was short-lived, this whiskey-inspired rebellion actually hastened the development of our national political parties. Americans began to line up behind two of the leading political factions of the time: Alexander Hamilton's Federalists, who were pushing for a stronger central government and looking out for the interests of the commercial class, and Thomas Jefferson's Democratic-Republicans, upholding states' rights and speaking for agrarian interests. Opposition to the Federalist party's policies began to take hold, often fomented in taverns by plying voters with liquor to sway their allegiance. So in many ways, alcohol played a role in helping to elect Thomas Jefferson in 1800, the first time in the United States that power shifted from one party to another. The irony here was that Jefferson himself hated whiskey and its effects on the American people—but he hated Hamilton's fiscal policies more.

By 1802, Jefferson had repealed the onerous whiskey tax. What hadn't been accomplished by battle was done by the ballot, aided by a steady supply of booze. Treating potential supporters to hard liquor became known as an infamous tactic of the Democrats, which Harry Croswell, that staunch Federalist, would confirm in his unintended public service of 1806 that first defined the cocktail in print.

THE ICE KING

Not long after the birth of the cocktail, a revolutionary new ingredient would again transform the way Americans drank: ice. Up to this point, frozen water was a luxury item, harvested from local lakes, ponds, and rivers and kept underground in ice houses. Ice had been used in punches, but was a scarce commodity when it came to cooling individual drinks. It was difficult to transport and keep through the summer, particularly in Southern cities. That all changed when young Bostonian Frederic Tudor almost single-handedly created a business around shipping ice. His success combined two early American signature traits: stubbornness and optimism. Well, maybe three—let's not forget a rapacious desire to get rich. Tudor's dream of cutting blocks of ice from Massachusetts ponds to cool libations around the world was first seen as folly. His original shipment to

Martinique mostly melted on the way there, and the rest disappeared soon after arrival because there was no place to store it. Which was just as well, because islanders had no idea how to use this newfangled ingredient. Tudor was undeterred, and as soon as he figured out the best way to ship and store it, he was delivering ice to Cuba, New Orleans, Charleston, and Savannah, to the delight of those perspiring drinkers. His crowning achievement was a successful shipment all the way to Calcutta in 1833. That made him famous worldwide, and helped cool countless British colonial gin and tonics.

Part of Tudor's ingenuity was knowing how to create demand for ice. Previously, Americans were just as happy to throw back their grogs and slings and cocktails warm. Tudor knew that once they got a taste of their drinks on the rocks, they wouldn't go back. All the way back in 1806, he had devised a plan to first give away his ice to taverns and saloons for free. "The object is to make the whole population use cold drinks instead of warm or tepid," he wrote in a letter. "A single conspicuous bar keeper ... selling steadily his liquors all cold without an increase in price, render it absolutely necessary that the others come to it or lose their customers." Once the habit was formed, Tudor would charge for refills—a move adopted by drug pushers the world over. Other entrepreneurs took note. One of his competitors dispatched Boston bartenders to London in 1842 to teach the Brits how to use ice in their cocktails. Pretty soon, even Queen Victoria was enjoying ice from Massachusetts. The global ice trade became so big and ubiquitous, that even Henry David Thoreau wrote in *Walden* about the harvesting of ice that disturbed his solitude during the winter months at the pond.

Ice became a preferred substitute for the water that was one of the four essential parts of the cocktail, and its slow delivery method forever changed Americans' drinking habits. Instead of throwing back raw liquor in a fiery gulp, they could linger over their individual drink, with the ice slowly mellowing the spirits and subtly changing the taste. Ice created classics like the Mint Julep and the Sherry Cobbler, and became an essential part of the American bar, where it was lovingly curated and carved. In today's craft cocktail bar, beautiful, perfectly clear, hand-cut orbs or squares of ice are almost required, a customer demand that has been resurrected from a century ago. The Ice King would be proud.

The ice trade had its king, but American bartenders still needed their Founding Father. They found one in Orsamus Willard, whom Wondrich called "the first celebrity bartender." Looking back, we might call him the George Washington of his craft, but in his day, he was dubbed the "Napoleon of bar-keepers." Willard held court at New York's famous City Hotel, a new style of establishment that was replacing traditional taverns. Indeed, the City Hotel was built on the ruins of the City Tavern, which was torn down to make way for this four-story, modern brick building.

Here, one of the main attractions was the bar, which was placed at the entrance to the hotel. The bar did double duty as the front desk, and the barkeeper was equal parts concierge and mixologist. A British naval officer mentioned the bar of the City Hotel in his 1826 travelogue, describing it disdainfully as a "buffet formed along the plan of a cage." For practical reasons, the spirits needed to be locked up when the bartender was away. But it appears that the ambidextrous Willard never left his perch, and was described as being there from dawn to dusk greeting guests and slinging drinks. His memory was legendary, and his bar was frequented by locals who talked politics over papers and travelers finding their way. As historian Christine Sismondo describes it in *America Walks Into a Bar*, visiting Willard at the City Hotel was seen as "a priceless souvenir from a trip to New York."

Willard was most famous for his perfectly prepared iced Mint Juleps, a skill taught to him by a Virginian who visited the hotel in 1817, and made possible because of Frederic Tudor's ice industry. (This is the same type of Mint Julep that was later introduced by Kentucky Senator Henry Clay to muggy Washington, D.C., at the famous Willard's Hotel—no relation to Orsamus—now known as The Willard Hotel.) Willard's name was even found in the newspapers his gentlemen patrons often read at the bar, which featured his recipe for the beloved Apple Toddy or columns praising his peach brandy punch—a drink he single handedly popularized in the 1830s.

There would be other well-known bartenders in this early era, like Sherwood E. "Shed" Sterling, dubbed the "Napoleon the Second of the Bar," who presided over New York's most famous luxury hotel of the era, the Astor House. Meanwhile, Peter Bent Brigham was creating a sensation at his Oyster Saloon in Boston, featuring long menus of fancy drinks with mysterious and humorous names. Instead of just calling out for a whiskey or gin cocktail or another one of the mixed drinks that had been around since colonial times, you could now order a Moral Suasion, a Pig and Whistle, or a Fiscal Agent while seated at his gentleman's bar. The Moral Suasion poked fun at Temperance advocates who tried to appeal to Americans' moral character to persuade them not to drink. This peach-brandy concoction was made to be so enticing that it could persuade abstainers to change their mind. Bartenders ever since have delighted in devising new and creative names for their cocktails.

David Wondrich has helped unearth other important bartending pioneers, giving a glimpse into the social complexity of the early American bar. Cato Alexander was a former slave living in New York City, working at inns when the city had a brief stint as our nation's capital, even tending to President Washington. As a free black man, he owned his own place called Cato's Tavern, just outside of the city limits (what is now the area around the United Nations building). He served the city's sporting set, and was well known for his juleps and cocktails. Bars existed as a sort of demimonde, where some African-Americans could cross racial barriers and work as bartenders or own their own establishments. Ironically, the South was often more hospitable to the black bartender, where they held the secret to gentlemen's clubs' punches and were recognized for their julep-crafting skills. Richmond-based bartender John Dabney even served one of his famous juleps to the future king of England. And while he was able to buy his and his wife's freedom from his earnings, he had no illusions about how tenuous his livelihood was under a dehumanizing system of slavery.

This was the case for Beverly Snow, an African-American and former slave who opened what was arguably Washington, D.C.'s first fine-dining restaurant, Snow's Epicurean Eating House. Abolition was becoming a contentious issue in the nation's capital, and there was a backlash on the gains made by free blacks after Nat Turner's Rebellion in 1831. An infamous race riot instigated by Washington's white working class, known as the Snow Riot of 1835, destroyed a number of free black-owned businesses in the capital, including Snow's restaurant. He and his family narrowly escaped and decamped to Canada, where he built a new restaurant in Toronto.

Wondrich has found examples of women behind the bar as well, including Martha Niblo, who helped run "Niblo's Garden" with her husband. It was a romantic, lantern-lit outdoor bar that would be just at home at its location today in modern SoHo. Martha was reportedly an expert at mixing drinks, creating delicious Sherry Cobblers piled high with ice and garnish that became a sensation during this period. Unfortunately, women bartenders became a rarer sight as the century progressed. While they had once been an integral part of running colonial American taverns and indeed supplying its beer and cider, women would increasingly be edged out of what were becoming male-only spaces: the hotel bar and the saloon.

The saloon in particular became a haven for men involved in the sporting life, with a penchant for card-playing, gambling, and horse-racing. It also developed into a place of spectacle and performance, not the least of which was the dexterity of the bartenders. Niblo's was where P.T. Barnum held his very first exhibit of curiosities in 1835. The curiosity in question was an elderly enslaved woman who was purportedly 161 years old, and billed as former nursemaid to an infant George Washington. Just a few months earlier, an unemployed Barnum had applied to be Niblo's barkeeper.

Inspired by the success of Willard and others who were professionalizing the craft at hotel bars, a new breed of bartenders began to make names for themselves in New York and other cities around the country. They even had a new name: mixologists. Correct: the moniker associated with a recent, hipster-infused craft cocktail revival actually has historical precedent. The term appeared in print as early as 1856, in a humorous essay in New York's *Knickerbocker Magazine*—though even that reference is a bit wry. The author Charles G. Leland recounts an overheard conversation between two uncouth Westerners in the next hotel room, referring to the establishment's bartender with reverence as a "mixologist of tipulars." It was meant as a joke, but as often happens, catchy terms catch on. It soon became an official moniker of the profession without a drop of irony.

AMERICAN DRINKERS

We've seen the evolution of bartenders during this period, but what about their customers? Probably no other American captures the evolution of our drinking habits during this period better than Edgar Allan Poe. He was born in Boston in 1809, just a few years after the cocktail first made its way into print. His father, David Poe, was a struggling actor who undoubtedly knew his way around the bars and saloons of his native Baltimore. He was also reportedly an alcoholic who abandoned his family when Edgar was just an infant, a predicament afflicting more and more American families. In 1826, the Presbyterian minister Lyman Beecher (father of *Uncle Tom's Cabin* author Harriet Beecher Stowe) delivered a series of famous sermons on intemperance and its effects in Boston. He co-founded the American Temperance Society, which within a few years would have chapters across the country. Its members pledged to swear off all ardent spirits except the holy one, and to use moral suasion to convince other Americans to do the same.

That same year, seventeen-year-old Poe was attending the newly opened University of Virginia, founded by Thomas Jefferson. The school was meant to be an idyllic "Academical Village" of the Enlightenment, but many of its first students were sons of wealthy Southern planters and merchants who had more interest in the sporting life than studying. Jefferson's ideals for the American citizen were hitting up against the reality of a new age. While Poe himself was a good student, he got caught up in the gambling and drinking that plagued the university in its early days. One of his classmates, Thomas Goode Tucker, wrote some fifty years later that Poe was "exceedingly fond of peach and honey," a punch made with the Southern favorite peach brandy. He also said that Poe "would seize a full glass, without water or sugar, and send it home at a single gulp." That sounds like the typical college shot, avoiding the other ingredients that would have made it a cocktail.

More than the drink, it was the gambling that was young Poe's undoing: he left the university after just one session because his foster father refused to pay his gambling debts and tuition. After a brief stint at West Point, Poe lived an itinerant writer's life that took him up and down the Eastern Seaboard of a country that was newly drenched in whiskey from the western states. When Andrew Jackson was elected in 1828 as a populist Democrat, his Western supporters practically mobbed the White House to celebrate. The crowd muddied the furniture, tipped over punch bowls, and practically crushed President Jackson in their attempt to shake his hand. While the president made his escape out the back, the mob was lured out of the White House with huge tubs of whiskey punch placed on the lawn outside.

British travelers were often the most insightful—if sometimes unreliable—witnesses to American drinking habits. Frances Trollope came to America in 1827, searching for a utopia of American equality and looking to make some money; what she found instead were "accents that breathe less of freedom than of onions and whiskey." Her *Domestic Manners of the Americans*, published in 1832 after she returned to England, bemoaned the free flow of cheap whiskey throughout the country, among a long list of other annoyances. Her book was a hit job on America—and an instant best seller. Predictably, it won her few friends this side of the Atlantic. But Trollope didn't care. She was already safely back in England when she penned her concluding verses about the Americans: "I do not like them. I do not like their principles, I do not like their manners, I do not like their opinions." Ironically, the one American thing she did seem to like had whiskey as its key ingredient: the Mint Julep.

Traveling English Captain Frederick Marryat also loved the Julep, and recorded his own recipe for one using peach brandy in his 1840 book *A Diary in America*. He even visited Fresh Pond in Massachusetts, remarking on the success of Frederic Tudor in harvesting the ice that would end up in his drink. Commenting on the drinking habits of the originators of the Julep, he wrote, "They say that you may always know the grave of a Virginian as from the quantity of Julep he has drunk mint invariably springs up where he has been buried." As for the rest of the country, he observed:

I'm sure the Americans can fix nothing without a drink. If you meet, you drink; if you part, you drink; if you make acquaintance, you drink; if you close a bargain, you drink; they quarrel in their drink, and they make it up with a drink. They drink, because it is hot; they drink, because it is cold. If successful in elections, they drink and rejoice; if not, they drink and swear;—they begin to drink early in the morning, they leave off late at night; they commence it early in life, and they continue it, until they soon drop into the grave. ... As for water, what the man said, when asked to belong to the

Temperance Society, appears to be the general opinion: "it's very good for navigation."

But temperance groups were proliferating throughout the country. One was started by a group of working-class heavy drinkers in their favorite Baltimore saloon. They called themselves the Washingtonian Temperance Society, and they swore off all alcohol for total sobriety. They did this by sharing their personal stories of how it had ruined their lives—an early precursor to Alcoholics Anonymous. Edgar Allan Poe himself would have had ample personal stories to share. He had a hard time avoiding drinking, even though he knew the bouts would leave him incapacitated for days. He would partake of the more refined Madeiras and clarets that were common in the higher social classes, and of course one of his most famous short stories involves a prized cask of Amontillado sherry. But he would eventually have a reputation as an incurable drinker of ardent spirits. One friend reported running into Poe at a bar in Baltimore in 1846, describing a drinking habit that hadn't seemed to change much since his college days. "[He] drank off a *big* whiskey, (I believe this was his favorite tipple) … I formed the opinion that the poet had, in his time, seen many a barkeeper's countenance …" In that same year, the *Knickerbocker Magazine* published a verse on Poe: "The crusty critic, all conjecture shames; / Nor shall the world know which the mortal sin, / Excessive genius or excessive gin!"

Near the end of his life, Poe himself joined a temperance society in Richmond and swore off all alcohol as he prepared to marry his recently widowed (and wealthy) childhood sweetheart. He disappeared on a trip to New York City, and was found delirious at a tavern in his native Baltimore. How he got there was unknown, but it was an election day and the bar was a polling place. Some scholars hypothesize today that he was caught up in a cooping scheme, in which unsuspecting citizens were plied with alcohol and then forced to vote in several different polling places. Poe died several days later, and the obituary confirmed the public's opinion that here was another man of promise brought low by alcohol.

In his 1855 autobiography, inveterate showman and entertainer P.T. Barnum wrote: "I saw so much intoxication among men of wealth and intellect, filling the highest positions in society, that I began to ask myself the question, What guarantee is there that I may not become a drunkard?"

He became a teetotaler instead, and put on a famous temperance play called *The Drunkard* at the American Museum, his house of wonders in New York City. He was buoyed by the Maine Law, passed in 1851 with the help of Portland mayor Neal Dow, which went further than any other temperance reforms. It outlawed the sale of all liquor except for medicinal and other non-fun purposes. Barnum wrote that instead of relying solely on moral suasion to curb drinking, "Our watchword now was, 'Prohibition!'"

While Barnum would only serve ice water in his museum, there was refreshment of a whole different sort being served in a saloon in the building's basement. There a young bartender named Jerry Thomas opened his first bar, the same year that the Maine Law passed. Thomas was a bit of a showman himself, having managed a minstrel troupe in California after traveling there as part of the Gold Rush, and then tending bar to thirsty '49ers. When he came back to New York, his theatrics were all behind the bar. After several stints slinging drinks at his own bars and at the famous Metropolitan Hotel, he did something that would cement his standing as the "Father of American Mixology."

In 1862, in the midst of the Civil War over that other great moral issue of the day—slavery—Jerry Thomas published the first American cocktail book, titled *How to Mix Drinks: Or, The Bon-Vivant's Companion*. It was a second defining moment for the cocktail, because it was the first time that recipes were published for the public. Over the next twenty years, Thomas became the superstar of American bartenders, and helped usher in a Golden Age of American-style drinking that would spread throughout the world.

OLD FASHIONED

This cocktail is the granddaddy of them all—and you might remember your grandpa and grandma drinking one. Although theirs was likely a sweeter and fruitier affair, with much of that fruit muddled into a pulp at the bottom and topped with an ersatz orange slice and a glowing maraschino cherry. This is the closest to the original Whiskey Cocktail recipe, though rye whiskey itself is a later addition. Like all of the earliest cocktails, you can actually make an Old Fashioned with whatever spirit you like. But lucky for us, we had a spicy, homegrown option in rye, which provides a perfect balance to this essential cocktail.

DOUBLE ROCKS GLASS (12-14 OZ.)

2 ounces rye whiskey
$\frac{1}{4}$–$\frac{1}{2}$ ounce rich simple syrup
(2 parts sugar to 1 part water)
2 dashes aromatic bitters (such as Angostura)
1 lemon peel, approximately 2 inches long
by $\frac{3}{4}$ of an inch wide, for garnish.

Combine whiskey, simple syrup, and bitters in a mixing glass or pint glass, add ice and stir until chilled. Strain into a double rocks glass, add new ice, and garnish with lemon peel. *Makes 1 drink.*

THE MINT JULEP

If you've ever had the pleasure of visiting the bar Revel in New Orleans and had esteemed bartender Chris McMillian make you a Mint Julep, you will never forget the rousing rendition he does of Kentucky Colonel Joshua Soule Smith's nineteenth-century ode to the drink. McMillian recites the poem from memory while using a large mallet to hammer ice inside of a Lewis bag (a canvas bag used for crushing ice). Not only is the drink strong and fragrant, but the poem puts you in a kind of trance, as a good Mint Julep (and good entertainer) should. Try to make yours with as much fanfare. A drink that draws its name from a thousand-year-old libation of roses and water from ancient Persia and is, as the poem goes, "the very dream of drinks," deserves as much.

JULEP CUP (14-16 OZ.)

6 sprigs mint, 3–4 for muddling and
remaining sprigs reserved for garnish
½ ounce rich simple syrup
(see recipe on page 60)
2 ounces bourbon whiskey

Muddle 3 to 4 mint sprigs with simple syrup in a julep cup. Remove mint after rubbing it around the cup's walls. Fill cup halfway with crushed ice and add bourbon. Fill cup the rest of the way with crushed ice and garnish with extra mint sprigs. *Makes 1 drink.*

SHERRY COBBLER

I happen to be a big fan of sherry, and think it was integral to drink-making in the United States. Yet if our discussion needed to be confined to one thing, it would be this: drink a Sherry Cobbler. It's a semisweet, low-alcohol treat that makes the summer bearable and can be repeated over and over again in a single sitting. You might hear how this drink popularized the straw in the nineteenth century, originally a natural reed, and later paper or metal (these are back in style now that the disposable plastic variety is déclassé). Or you might hear odes to how beautifully it's decorated, with a lovely summit of seasonal fruit and mint. Never mind all that—I still think its single greatest attribute, besides tasting great, is how sessionable it is. Pour yourself another!

HIGHBALL GLASS (12-14 OZ.)

2 ounces Oloroso sherry
½ ounce rich simple syrup
(see recipe on page 60)
1 orange wheel, cut in half and muddled
½ orange wheel, mint sprig, and seasonal berries
(raspberries, blueberries, chopped strawberries)
for garnish

Shake sherry and simple syrup with 2 muddled half wheels of orange and ice. Strain into glass. Top with crushed ice. Garnish with additional half orange wheel, mint sprig, and seasonal berries. Serve with a straw.

Makes 1 drink.

SAZERAC

If you've read this far, you already know that the Sazerac was not the first cocktail.
If you turned immediately to this page, I'm sorry to tell you, especially if you're from New Orleans, that it's not even remotely true. Yet the Sazerac deserves all the attention it gets. It's a fine blending of ingredients that is virtually unparalleled in any other whiskey drink. It is what would happen if you melted down a combination of silk and iron, or diamonds with concrete. Everything harsh or strong about whiskey, bitters, and absinthe are subsumed within the greater whole, and made not just palatable, but smooth, beautiful, and balanced.
You may wish to adjust the sugar and bitters to your taste, but try not to stray too far. This drink is carefully constructed and does not need you meddling with it.

ROCKS GLASS (10-12 OZ.)

2 ounces rye whiskey
¼ ounce simple syrup (one part sugar to one part water)
3 dashes Peychaud's Bitters
Splash of absinthe for rinse (less than bar spoon)
Lemon peel

Fill rocks glass with ice. In a mixing glass, add whiskey, simple syrup, bitters, and ice, and stir until cold. Dump ice from first glass and rinse with absinthe by pouring a splash and swirling to coat glass, pouring out any excess. Strain contents of mixing glass into rocks glass. Express oils from lemon peel by holding the exocarp (outside of peel) by both ends and twisting over the drink. Discard peel. *Makes 1 drink*.

LOST BOYS COCKTAIL (ORIGINAL)

Using the Old Fashioned as a starting point is a no-brainer, as it is the OG cocktail. And there are plenty of ways to invent new (and sometimes better) versions. With the Lost Boys, I just thought of flavors I loved: smoky scotch, rich chocolate, sweet orange, and syrupy honey. It came together effortlessly. The name is not derived from the 1980s teenage heartthrob vampire movie though. It was created for Kelly Muccio and her store in Georgetown, Washington, D.C., called Lost Boys. She would suit men who maybe did not have as much up on style as they did social leverage (they paid top dollar for her styling). In that way, this was designed as a masculine cocktail. Though don't let that fool you—anyone can drink it, and should.

DOUBLE ROCKS GLASS (12-14 OZ.)

2 ounces blended Scotch (as opposed to a single malt)
½ ounce honey syrup (2 parts honey to 1 part water)
Dash Bittermens Xocolatl Mole Bitters
Dash orange bitters
Orange peel for garnish

To make honey syrup, heat water and add honey, stirring until thoroughly blended. Allow to cool before using. Combine Scotch, honey syrup, and bitters in a mixing glass. Add ice and stir. Strain into double rocks glass over ice cubes. Garnish with orange peel.

Makes 1 drink.

CHAPTER THREE

Martini
p80

THE GOLDEN AGE

1860s>1910s

It's hard to imagine just how revolutionary the creation of the cocktail was. So revolutionary that it exists, to this day, as one of America's greatest culinary creations and exports. Once, a friend who was having a drink in Chile texted me to say how awful his cocktail was. He'd asked for an Old Fashioned and, in exchange, he got a drink filled with fruit, including pineapple. The original Old Fashioned, as we've learned, is the closest we can get to the original, stripped-down cocktail. There should be no fruit salad at the bottom, unless you order it in Milwaukee, which has adopted the muddled orange and cherry version as its own. And there should most certainly be no trace of pineapple—that addition would be a monstrous sin to Old Fashioned purists, whether they be in Chile or Chicago.

Though I could sympathize with my friend's plight, I think the greater point is this: he got an Old Fashioned. The drink has become so recognizable that it is produced just about anywhere in the world. Whether it is good is something altogether different. Cocktails have also become so ubiquitous that they have even become a catchall term for just about any drink. I've been to a cocktail party more than once where the "cocktails" included wine and highballs. The original meaning of cocktail in the nineteenth century was something fairly specific—not just any alcoholic beverage, but that magical combination of just four ingredients—spirit, sugar, water, and bitters. Early bartender guides generally distinguished cocktails from sours, flips, punches, and cobblers and a whole slew of different drinks, let alone Chardonnay and Vodka Soda.

The unknown person who created the perfect combination of ingredients found in a cocktail surely did not realize exactly what magic he or she had created, and that it would become something far beyond his or her wildest imagination. Not just in terms of its ubiquity but *why* it became ubiquitous. The cocktail is the perfect foil for invention and replication, the DNA of drinking. The wave of professional bartenders that followed soon realized they had struck a different kind of gold than the precious metal found in California. In his foreword to a 1926 book on Washington, D.C. bartender Henry William Thomas, publisher Charles V. Wheeler called the cocktail a "triumph of contradiction," adding:

> You put in a little syrup to make it sweet and a squeeze of lemon to make it sour; a jigger of rum to make it hot and a bit of ice to make it cold; then you shoot a squirt of heavenly fizz and a dash of hellish bitters; all has to be well shaken up to make it settle down so that it will quench the thirst and, (oh yes!) invite another; thus cheering you on your way as you linger a while. Well—that's the way it goes!

This isn't exactly the formula we see in the 1806 definition. But by the late nineteenth century, the cocktail had greatly expanded its ingredients and redoubled its permutations. While America itself was being torn asunder by the Civil War, the country was entering a Golden Age of cocktails. Jerry Thomas's 1862 *Bar-Tenders Guide*, which kicks off the era, featured a mere ten cocktails. By his 1887 reprint, cocktails had nearly doubled to nineteen (twenty if you include a soda cocktail, which I don't). And by the turn of the century, there were hundreds of cocktails and mixed drinks for discerning drinkers to choose from, each more elaborate and fancy than the last. But there was a trinity of drinks from the Golden Age that would soon enter the cocktail pantheon: the Manhattan, Martini, and Daiquiri.

FROM MANHATTAN TO MARTINEZ

The Manhattan has a rather convoluted history and enough origin myths to fill an entire book—in fact, author Phil Greene did just that with *The Manhattan: The Story of the First Modern Cocktail*. I won't spoil the ending, but I will say that he chronicles how the addition of aromatized wine (aka vermouth) changed the Old Fashioned into a modern cocktail, the Manhattan. The sweetener of sugar is replaced by vermouth, and the whole concoction is stirred and strained into a cocktail glass. Elegant stemware replaces the bulky rocks glass, a shimmering burnt-amber color replaces the murky brown, and a taut surface replaces a submerged miniature iceberg to become a triumph of contradictions as well as one of pleasing visual aesthetics. The influence of the Manhattan doesn't end there. It has impeccable genes, which it passed on to a drink called the Martinez, and eventually the Martini.

In O.H. Byron's *The Modern Bartenders' Guide*, the author announces as much. After detailing not one but two recipes for the Manhattan, he writes this under the heading for the Martinez: "Same as Manhattan, only you substitute gin for whisky." I realize that the Martinez sounds like the Manhattan's south-of-the border cousin, but it was likely created in the United States. The city of Martinez, California, claims its birth, and, by proxy, the origination of the Martini. In a version that's become city lore, a miner stopped in Martinez on his way back to San Francisco in 1849 after striking it rich during the Gold Rush. He headed straight for a bar intending to celebrate with champagne. Instead the bartender served up what he called a "Martinez Special," one part dry Sauterne wine, three parts gin, stirred with ice and served with an olive. The miner recalled the recipe back in San Francisco where it caught on. And perhaps if you say "Martinez" enough times, and after enough drinks, it morphs into "Martini."

I think we can take that one with a grain of salt, but the idea that the Martinez is the progenitor of the Martini is a conclusion other cocktail writers and historians have advanced with credible evidence. First of all, despite the fact that we have learned to order very dry Martinis, sometimes omitting the vermouth all together—a practice I cannot stand behind— there exists a less dry version of the Martini using a sweeter style of gin called Old Tom Gin and sweet vermouth. Replace the sweet gin and sweet vermouth with dry gin and dry vermouth and the Dry Martini emerges.

The Martinez is a wonderful drink, and one that doesn't just form the missing link between the Manhattan and Martini in a historical sense—it really tastes as though the two drinks were swirled together in a soft-serve machine. It has the richness of a Manhattan and the sharp, botanical finish of a Martini. Shortly after the Martinez appears, the Martini cocktail also shows up in a variety of forms. The first mention of the Martini recipe is in Harry Johnson's 1888 reprint of his *New and Improved Bartenders' Manual*:

Fill up the glass with ice;

2 or 3 dashes of Gum Syrup;

2 or 3 dashes of Bitters; (Boker's genuine only.)

1 dash of Curaçoa;

½ wine glassful of Old Tom Gin;

½ wine glassful of Vermouth;

Stir up well with a spoon, strain it into a fancy cocktail glass, squeeze a peel of lemon on top, and serve.

Compare this to the recipe for the Martinez in Jerry Thomas's 1887 reprint of *Bar-Tenders Guide*:

Take 1 dash of Boker's bitters.

2 dashes of Maraschino.

1 pony of Old Tom gin.

1 wine glass of Vermouth.

2 small lumps of ice.

Shake up thoroughly, and strain into a large cocktail glass. Put a quarter of a slice of lemon in the glass, and serve. If the guest prefers it very sweet, add two dashes of gum syrup.

The difference between the two, besides one being stirred and the other being shaken (perhaps the original battle between shaken and stirred!), is Curaçao instead of maraschino and a slightly different ratio of ingredients. The early Martini's first iteration has equal parts, but this soon morphs into a variety of different ratios, whereas the Martinez remains 2:1. Then comes the Dry Martini, the very perfection of cocktail—what some anonymous poet referred to as "satin, fire, and ice; Fred Astaire in a glass; surgical cleanliness, insight, comfort; redemption and absolution."

THE KING OF COCKTAILS

The Dry Martini first appears in its earthly form—people like me consider it divine in origin—in a few different iterations. There is the 1900 mention

in Harry Johnson's manual of the Marguerite cocktail, which features
equal parts dry gin and dry vermouth, orange bitters, and anisette. Then
there is the Puritan cocktail in Frederic L. Knowles's *The Cocktail Book:
A Sideboard Manual for Gentlemen* in 1901, which is a gin-to-vermouth ratio
of 2:1, with a spoonful of yellow chartreuse. The Olivette cocktail found in
John Applegreen's 1904 *Bar Book* is equal parts gin and vermouth, with the
addition of Peychaud's. And finally there is the very first mention of the
phrase "Dry Martini" in a French bartender's manual titled *American-Bar
Recettes des Boissons Anglaises et Américaines*, featuring equal parts gin and
vermouth, with orange bitters and a cherry, olive, or lemon peel. But the
one I land on as the true progenitor, because it mirrors the French version
without dillydallying about what garnish to choose, is the Crisp Cocktail,
also from *Applegreen's Bar Book*, which is equal parts gin and vermouth,
with orange bitters and lemon peel, stir and strain.

Now, a quick note about the Dry Martini. There is no use in my playing the
objective observer here. This is my favorite cocktail and thus the very best
cocktail that exists. It's all about clean lines and rich texture, the interplay
of savage and subtle flavors, how the juniper sneaks up on you when it is
properly chilled so as to freeze your lip, the lemon aroma that pulls on your
nose. All of this marks a moment, I believe, in history when we reached
a zenith in cocktail making. Many great cocktails are to follow, but none
that rival the Martini for the title of King of Cocktails. All the forms I've
mentioned feed into this one like a river to the source. But the one form
it doesn't appear in is as a Vodka Martini, at least not until much later,
and then it was titled the Kangaroo Cocktail. So for those who came here
to debate, let's put an end to it right now: martinis are made with gin.
To distinguish a "martini" with vodka you must use the modifier "vodka,"
as in "Vodka Martini." Also, you should be ashamed of yourself.

EL DAIQUIRI

The third cocktail of our holy trinity of the Golden Era is the Daiquiri.
It first made its appearance in Cuba, recorded by an American engineer
named Jennings Cox just before the Spanish-American War. This rum-based
cocktail isn't the Daiquiri of the strawberry persuasion that is most often
dispensed from a slushie machine or available at a drive-through window
in New Orleans. It's a simple combination of rum, limes, and sugar. It's

technically classified as a sour, but today it's commonly grouped in the greater category of cocktail.

While the creation of the Daiquiri is ascribed to Cox, drinks made of rum, citrus, and honey or sugar were already commonly served in Cuba. However, his story is the one written down, which gives us the precise measurements of the Daiquiri. Jennings arrived in Cuba in 1895 working for the Spanish American Iron Ore Company, which had mines near the port village of Daiquirí. He was thought to have made his version of the drink when he was entertaining American guests and ran out of gin. Rather than serve the local Bacardi rum straight, he added limes and sugar, an improvisation that has spawned many a good cocktail.

The village of Daiquirí was where American troops would land just a couple years later to help Cuban rebels overthrow the Spanish government. President McKinley had been pressured into the Spanish-American War by the New York press, particularly after the mysterious explosion of the *U.S.S. Maine* in Havana Harbor. (This incident inspired the name for another cocktail, Remember the Maine.) Daiquiri became the name of Cox's cocktail that would in turn take America by storm. The drink makes its first appearance in the United States at the Army and Navy Club in Washington, D.C., in 1909. Admiral Lucius Johnson had tasted it in Cuba and loved it so much that he brought it home with him. There, in the Army and Navy Club's Daiquiri Lounge, still hangs a plaque commemorating the drink.

About fifty years later, it would become the favorite cocktail of former Navy officer John F. Kennedy, who as president would be pressured into supporting an invasion of Cuba. While this one was not a success and America would be estranged from Cuba for at least another fifty years, we would still hold the Daiquiri close to our hearts and to our lips.

THE IDEAL BARTENDER

The proliferation of cocktails and fancy drinks reached their pinnacle during the Golden Age, and so did the cult of the celebrity bartender, exemplified by the legendary Jerry Thomas. He cut quite the figure behind the bar, adorned with glittering diamonds and sporting a pair of pet white rats who would perch on his shoulders as he mixed drinks. One of those drinks, his signature Blue Blazer, was lit on fire to create a flaming arch of whiskey as he poured it from one metal tin to another. Suffice to say, he had a flair for the theatrical. He had a big personality and was a man of the world, so admired and respected by his patrons that he was nicknamed "The Professor." Two more emerged alongside him to form a triumvirate, what spirits maker and cocktail expert Simon Ford dubbed the "Three Amigos" of the Golden Age: Jerry Thomas, Harry Johnson, and William "The Only William" Schmidt.

They had many traits in common, besides their impressive mustaches. They were well traveled, hopping from growing American cities like San Francisco, St. Louis, Chicago, and New Orleans, and even traveling through Europe before settling in New York. They all published their own influential bartending guides—Johnson's was *The New and Improved Bartender's Manual*, and Schmidt's was *The Flowing Bowl: What and When to Drink*. They all died in reduced circumstances after riding a wave of fame and prosperity—the bartending life could be a tough one, after all. And when they passed, glowing obituaries would testify to their miraculous mixology, undoubtedly written by journalists who knew the fact firsthand.

Despite their similarities—or because of them—these amigos were not necessarily friends. Harry Johnson in particular was a longtime rival of Jerry Thomas. They met in San Francisco in the 1860s, when the city was still a raw town reveling in the reflected aura of gold, and the cocktails were just as precious. Everything from Champagne to whiskey to Peruvian pisco were free flowing—and you might find promising upstarts like a young Mark Twain at the bar, trading tall tales with his firefighter friend Tom Sawyer. (Sawyer would go on to open his own bar in the city, and would advertise on the sign out front that he was the namesake of one of America's most famous literary inventions.)

Harry Johnson would also claim that he made literary history in San Francisco by publishing America's first bartending manual, beating Thomas's 1862 book. That would have been quite the feat, considering Johnson reportedly arrived in San Francisco in 1861 as an ex-sailor nursing a broken arm. If it existed, no one ever saw the manuscript, nor the award for America's best bartender he claimed he won in a prestigious competition in

New Orleans several years later. Despite the tendency toward extreme self-promotion, his bartending manual is still a classic today. In his day, it was the first book to include not only recipes on how to make drinks, but advice on how to be an ideal bartender. He pioneered that now venerable position of bar consultant, a trend continued by today's superstar mixologists.

As Twain put it, "The cheapest and easiest way to become an influential man and be looked up to by the community at large, was to stand behind a bar, wear a cluster-diamond pin, and sell whisky." He was talking about the rough-and-tumble culture of 1870s Nevada, but the profession became a stepping-stone for many an upstart. As the Golden Age progressed, bartending was seen as an elevated and noble calling, requiring years of training and apprenticeship. It wasn't equal opportunity though. Women bartenders became a rare sight in America during this period. And yet in some areas of the country, black bartenders were able to chart a path toward upward economic mobility, despite enforced segregation and Jim Crow laws.

Dick Francis was born to free parents in Virginia, and tended bar at the famous saloon Hancock's in Washington, D.C. for more than thirty-five years, both before and after the Civil War. The place was just around the corner from the White House at the fortuitous address of 1234 Pennsylvania Avenue, and was known as the Old Curiosity Shop because of the odd assortment of national memorabilia—everything from esteemed generals' swords and pistols to what was purported to be Zachary Taylor's hat and George Washington's slippers. Francis likely served customers as disparate as Henry Clay and John Wilkes Booth, because just about everyone stopped in at Hancock's. Near the end of his life in the 1880s, Francis took a well-paid post as manager of the restaurant and bar in the U.S. Senate. With his earnings from behind the bar and savvy real estate investments in the District, he was able to send his son to medical school and secure a place in the middle class for his family.

David Wondrich and D.C. bartender Duane Sylvestre have helped reclaim the stories of Dick Francis and others during this period, including re-discovering the existence of the Colored Mixologists Club, a guild of African-American bartenders working in Washington to elevate the profession. In 1917, Tom Bullock, the St. Louis Country Club's bartender, became the first African American to publish a cocktail manual. Titled

The Ideal Bartender, it came with an introduction from local luminary and club member George Herbert Walker. The name might sound familiar—his grandson would be future President George Herbert Walker Bush.

Bullock's drinks even got a former president in a spot of trouble. In a 1913 libel case centered on his alleged drinking habits, Teddy Roosevelt testified that he had only taken a few sips of a Mint Julep at the St. Louis Country Club since leaving the presidency. The *St. Louis Post-Dispatch* was having none of it, editorializing that no one could resist finishing one of Bullock's masterful Juleps. But just three years after he published his cocktail manual, Tom Bullock and other black bartenders would no longer have a legal profession. All of their hard-fought gains would disappear with the onset of Prohibition.

A PRELUDE TO THE END

In the early twentieth century, the cocktail was already an American icon. The Manhattan, Martini, and Daiquiri had all become ascendant. The bar scene was booming, and bartenders stood tall as celebrities in their time. The cocktail even became one of our most famous exports, as "American Bars" began to spring up around the world serving cocktails in London, Paris, and Venice. The cocktail had come a long way since a simple hangover remedy from 1803.

It was a great time to be a drinker, and Americans fully took advantage of their liberties. But what was soon to come would knock the wind out of the sails of America's cocktail revolution. As Americans imbibed with unrestrained glee, the forces of temperance were marshalling. The Women's Christian Temperance Union organized protests of women to sit outside saloons and pray for men's souls as they imbibed. The extremist Carrie Nation took it one step further. Claiming divine inspiration, she began to take a hatchet to beautiful mahogany bars in the name of the Holy Spirit. Her self-described "hatchetations" led many saloons to post a sign reading "All Nations Welcome But Carrie." These protests morphed into a politically savvy movement to pass one of the most impressive pieces of legislation against civil freedoms. It would cause such a stir, no pun intended, that it ended up adding two amendments to the Constitution. Quite a feat considering how so few have passed.

In Washington, D.C., ground zero for the temperance battle, a Texas senator named Morris Sheppard passed the Sheppard Bone-Dry Act (yes, that was its official name). Starting in 1917, it outlawed booze in the District a full two years before nationwide legislation enacted Prohibition. It was meant to send a message and set an example of the bibulous capital that was famous for its drinking dens. One such den, Shoomaker's, served up to the very last hour. Its customers—the judges, congressmen, and statesmen of the time—sang in the street as the bar closed. The song they purportedly sang was a popular, patriotic tune of the time, "Over There." Its famous refrain, "The Yanks are coming ...," would signal the beginning of the end for legal drinking in the States, but it was an omen for what was to come next for the cocktail and its makers. They would either have to move underground or find a new home overseas.

MANHATTAN

This is the one drink that hung on after classic cocktails disappeared. But should it have? My love for the Manhattan is simple: It is the grandfather of the Martini, my favorite drink. Beyond that, I have never cared much for them. However, I know how many of you feel, so here is the secret to improve your Manhattan: Use a good rye whiskey. That is this drink's only saving grace: quality booze. When made with bourbon or cheap whiskey, it is an unfathomable mess—soft, sweet, and insipid, reminiscent of cherry juice or ice cream. Nine times out of ten I prefer my whiskey neat. The tenth time, I pray you used the good stuff.

COCKTAIL GLASS (5.5-7.5 OZ.)

2 ounces rye whiskey
1 ounce sweet vermouth
Dash aromatic bitters
Brandied cherry for garnish

Add all ingredients to a mixing glass, and stir with ice until cold.
Strain into chilled cocktail glass and garnish with a brandied cherry.
Makes 1 drink.

MARTINEZ

This drink has been nothing short of revelatory to me. Not only does it meld the Martini and the Manhattan in an inspired twist, but it has become one of my favorite cocktails to drink with meals. While I was working as a sommelier, I was tasked with matching a wine to a pickle plate. For wine aficionados, you know this is no small feat, since the vinegar doesn't play well with wine. I decided to try a cocktail and the Martinez seemed a reasonable start. The pairing was successful, and opened my eyes to the power of cocktail pairings.

COCKTAIL GLASS (5.5-7.5 OZ.)

1 ½ ounces Old Tom gin
1 ½ ounces sweet vermouth
2 dashes orange bitters
1 bar spoon (about 1 teaspoon) Maraschino liqueur
1 lemon peel (approximately 2 inches long by ¾ of an inch wide) for garnish

Combine liquid ingredients in a mixing glass. Add ice and stir until cold. Strain into chilled cocktail glass, express the peel of the lemon over the top, and add peel to drink. *Makes 1 drink.*

MARTINI

In 2010, *GQ* magazine claimed I made the best Martini in America. Who am I to argue with that? But I think that people usually make the drink they like the best with the most care. I freeze the gin, refrigerate the vermouth, carefully stir the mix, then use a thermometer to make sure the drink is 29°F. I realize this is OCD Martini-making behavior, but you should try it. The other secret to the technique is to practice stirring with intention and care. Japanese bartender Kazuo Uyeda described the act of stirring as weaving together threads of silk. If your elbow is flailing, and liquid is being splashed about like an orca at Seaworld, you are doing it wrong. Stop, place the bar spoon between your pointer and middle finger. Gently glide the back end of the spoon around the edges of the mixing glass. It should be quiet, meditative, and elegant to watch.

COCKTAIL GLASS (5.5-7.5 OZ.)

1 ½ ounces dry gin
1 ½ ounces dry vermouth
Dash Orange bitters
Lemon peel for garnish

Combine ingredients in mixing glass and stir with ice until very cold. Strain into chilled cocktail glass, express a lemon peel overtop (do not rub the lemon on rim), and discard peel. *Makes 1 drink.*

DAIQUIRI

We have discussed the history of the Daiquiri, but perhaps it would be good to add something more recent: the DTO. DTO stands for Daiquiri Time Out, created by Andrew Dietz, who lobbied the Boston cocktail community to make it a greeting and celebration among bartenders. I first learned of it through bartender extraordinaire, Jackson Cannon. There are a few ways to do it but the basic idea is to make a classic Daiquiri and share it with other bartenders, revelers, or cocktail enthusiasts. You can make several full-sized drinks, but more often one drink is made, split among several shot glasses, and served to the group. It is about being present and enjoying the love of a good drink—and a Daiquiri is a damn good drink.

COCKTAIL GLASS (5.5-7.5 OZ.)

2 ounces white rum
¾ ounces lime juice
½ ounces rich simple syrup (see recipe on page 60)

Combine ingredients with ice and shake until cold.

Strain into chilled glass. *Makes 1 drink.*

STEADY COCKTAIL
(ORIGINAL)

This Martini variant is named after the motto of the Carthusian monks who make Elixir Vegetal: *Stat crux dum volvitur orbis* (Latin for, "The cross is steady while the world is turning."). I suppose it was also named such in hope that the ground stays steady as you drink them, if you know what I mean. You may have trouble getting your hands on a bottle of Elixir Vegetal de la Grande-Chartreuse, as it's not currently imported in the United States. Try harder, it's worth it. The aroma is like falling into a garden. However, if you aren't visiting France anytime soon, use a barspoon of green Chartreuse instead.

COCKTAIL GLASS (5.5-7.5 OZ.)

1 ½ ounces dry gin
1 ½ ounces dry vermouth
2 dashes Elixir Vegetal de la Grande-Chartreuse
(or a scant barspoon of green Chartreuse)

Combine ingredients in a mixing glass or pint glass, add ice, and stir until cold. Strain into chilled cocktail glass. Do not garnish.

Makes 1 drink.

CHAPTER FOUR

Scofflaw
p96

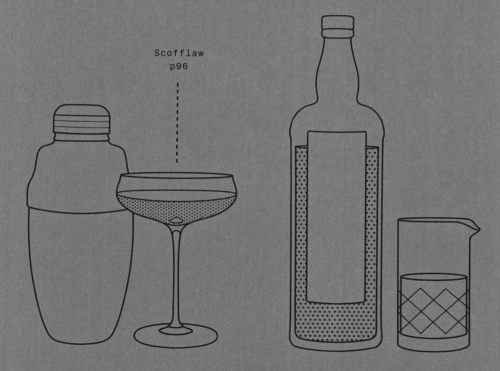

LOST GENERATION

1920s > 1930s

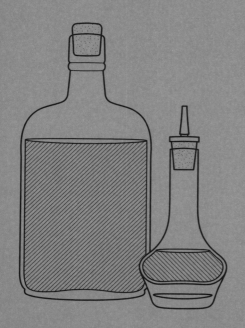

So here we are. And it's not like we didn't see it coming.
The temperance movement had been a part of America
since nearly the beginning of the country. Its growth
followed the rise of the cocktail on almost parallel
paths. It gained strength with the abolitionist cause and
with women's suffrage, at a time when temperance was
considered by many to be an equally progressive policy
to address the social ills that came with alcohol abuse.
But it also fed on Americans' fears of who should be able
to drink, channeling racial prejudice and anti-immigrant
sentiment. Groups like the Women's Christian Temperance
Union and the Anti-Saloon League pioneered single-issue
advocacy and culture-war tactics that would be familiar
to our politics today. And they managed a seemingly
insurmountable task—an amendment to the Constitution
to actually take American freedom away. It must have
been surreal to drinkers and bartenders when it actually
happened. Just as drinking in America had gotten really,
really good, the Prohibition era was upon us.

The nation's last call came on January 17, 1920, when Prohibition officially
went into effect throughout the country. What was originally intended
to target just hard liquor ended up banning the manufacture and sale of
practically every alcoholic beverage, including wine and beer. California's
vines were ripped out of the ground or converted into making grape juice.
Small breweries around the country went out of business, with the larger
ones shifting to producing ice or "soft drinks," the term that differentiated
nonalcoholic beverages from "hard" alcoholic drinks.

So what did this mean for cocktails? Nothing good. The complex recipes
and ingredients that flourished in the Golden Age would be lost to time

as the bartending profession became illegal. For mixologists, this was their career and livelihood on the line. They had to either shift to another trade or go abroad to continue to ply their skills at American-style bars around the world. In terms of the destruction of the country's cultural and culinary heritage, Prohibition was like the phylloxera, the American mite that nearly wiped out the entire wine industry in Europe. Except this was something we did to ourselves.

Key ingredients of the cocktail would vanish from American shores. The bitters market had already suffered a huge setback in 1906, when the Pure Food and Drug Act came into effect. Bitters had multiplied throughout the nineteenth century, with some purporting outrageous curative claims, although they were little better than snake oil. That act regulated most of the bitters makers out of business, and Prohibition dealt a blow to the remaining reputable companies. The bitters business went from hundreds of different brands to basically just a few. The two largest brands were the ones we know today: Angostura and Peychaud's. But other common bitters like Abbott's and Boker's Bitters, which appear in early cocktail recipes from Jerry Thomas and the like, were rendered extinct. (Fortunately they have been resurrected by craft producers.)

Prohibition also narrowed the cocktail field considerably. Out were the drinks that included complex mixtures of imported liqueurs and aged spirits. In were simpler concoctions with whiskey or gin and lots of sweetener to cover up the inferior booze, whether it was fruit juice, maraschino, grenadine, or simple syrup. The drinks that fared the best were the quickest and easiest to make, considering just making them was an illegal act. That included highballs, which is basically any base spirit over ice and filled with a mixer (soda water, ginger ale, Coke, etc.) and their close cousin, the Rickey.

THE RICKEY

When the patrons at Washington's famous Shoomaker's made their last toasts, they probably threw back a few Rickeys. The drink had been invented there, after all. The rickey is a category of mixed drinks made from a base spirit, little or no sugar, and half of a lime squeezed and dropped in the glass, all topped with carbonated water. And it's all perfectly fitting that a lobbyist is credited, although erroneously, with the creation of D.C.'s indigenous cocktail: Colonel Joe Rickey. He was an influential and colorful Democratic lobbyist from Missouri who was a regular patron of Shoomaker's and later its owner.

Shoomaker's was considered Washington's original dive bar, just off Pennsylvania Avenue a few blocks from the White House, and on a stretch of street nicknamed "Rum Row" for all of the other saloons surrounding it. It was also just a block away from "Newspaper Row," which ensured a steady clientele of journalist drinkers. Patrons described a bar crowded with political artifacts and mementos, as well as dust and cobwebs. "Shoomaker's is a grocery—a wet grocery—where no groceries have been sold since Lee surrendered to Grant," wrote artist and philosopher Elbert Hubbard after a visit there. "Outside, the place is guiltless of paint, and the architecture is an eyesore to the surrounding neighbors. . . The shabbiness of the place is its asset; the cobwebs are its charm."

There was said to be so much history here that the bartenders refused to clean it. One porter was purportedly fired for wiping down a table, with the admonition about the generations of luminaries whose elbows had rested on that very surface. Shoomaker's originally opened in 1858, and hosted just about every reporter, politician, and future president to come through Washington, except for Rutherford B. Hayes, who would ban alcohol from the White House. First Lady Lucy Hayes was a famous teetotaler and supporter of temperance, which later earned her the nickname of "Lemonade Lucy."

Perhaps that's why the capital needed a new cocktail all its own. The Rickey came onto the scene just after Hayes left office. The most accepted origin story of the Rickey goes that Shoomaker's bartender George A. Williamson combined his boss Colonel Rickey's favorite bourbon with mineral water and the juice and shell of half a lime. That may have been influenced by another patron who had visited the Caribbean and commented how drinks there, such as the Swizzle, included lime juice and the shell. Nothing too complicated, but it seems to have caught on, and soon Washingtonians were throwing them back with regularity. This summertime sipper has been called air conditioning in a glass, which was perfect for the muggy Washington summers when the only form of air conditioning was a front porch. But it

088

would go on to become a worldwide sensation when mixed with gin. The Rickey was once so popular that in a 1907 *Los Angeles Herald* article titled "Limes Are On Time," the writer celebrated the arrival of a shipment of two million limes from the West Indies as the raw materials for Gin Rickeys: "Now let the warm weather come and let the siphons hiss, because the limes are here ready for the gin rickeys."

When Prohibition went into effect, Shoomaker's tried to change with the times by using the siphon without the gin and converting to a soda fountain shop. That only lasted a few months. The loyal customers never returned, and soon the immortal Shoomaker's was no more. But the Rickey lived on—although admittedly it was living a double life. Minus the booze, it became a famous temperance soft drink, served at soda fountains across the country. But the Gin Rickey was an equally popular Prohibition cocktail because it was easy to make and featured a lot of lime (and maybe some sugar) to cover up the harshness of what was likely bathtub gin. It was one of F. Scott Fitzgerald's favorite drinks, and even makes an appearance in *The Great Gatsby*, where the characters drink them in "long, greedy swallows" to combat the summer heat. Of course we know how that story ended, both for Gatsby and Fitzgerald, who died at the age of 44 after two decades of hard living.

And what happened to Colonel Joe Rickey? He was made famous worldwide for a drink he actually didn't care for very much. He still preferred his drink with bourbon or rye whiskey, and a touch of lemon instead of lime. He left politics for business and Washington for New York, got into the soda water industry that was the basis of his eponymous drink, and then got into debt. He died in 1903 after drinking a decidedly different kind of cocktail of his own making: whiskey mixed with carbolic acid.

AMERICA'S WETTEST CITY

Americans famously flouted Prohibition laws, with speakeasies cropping up in cities big and small, and illicit bootlegging leading to a rise in organized crime in places like New York, Boston, Atlantic City, and Chicago. It would have been no surprise to Colonel Joe Rickey that his adopted hometown of Washington was one of the biggest flouters. As a lobbyist, he was used to our lawmakers voting one way and acting another.

President Woodrow Wilson had tried to veto the Volstead Act, which was the strict law that allowed the government to enforce Prohibition. It famously overreached by outlawing beer and wine (Thomas Jefferson would have been appalled)—basically anything over .5 percent alcohol. Congress overrode his veto, and soon Wilson himself was subject to the act's massive reach: he had to get special permission to move his extensive wine collection from the White House to his retirement home two miles away. The next president, Warren Harding, didn't bother asking for permission. He brought his liquor with him into the White House and would famously drink there with his political allies while the rest of Washington was supposed to be dry.

Only it wasn't. Historian Garrett Peck details just how wet with booze the nation's capital had become in his book *Prohibition in Washington, D.C.: How Dry We Weren't*. The biggest offenders were at the other end of Pennsylvania Avenue. Members of Congress themselves had a number of bootleggers supplying them with booze. One of the most famous was known as "The Man in the Green Hat." His real name was George Cassiday, and he was a well-known sight walking throughout the Capitol building with his green felt hat. Peck describes how bootlegging in our nation's capital was different from the lawbreaking in other cities. There was no organized crime, like Capone's gang in Chicago that rose to power through the illegal alcohol trade. People like Cassiday were on the payroll of the lawmakers themselves. The Man in the Green Hat actually set up shop in the basement of one of the House office buildings to make it easier to distribute the booze. When he was caught one day and banned from the House, he simply moved over to the Senate side and set up shop there.

His arrangement lasted for ten years, almost the entire length of the Prohibition era. When he was finally arrested in 1930, he published an exposé in the *Washington Post* to tell Americans just how dry their representatives weren't. He estimated that four out of five members of Congress were his customers, that same proportion who had voted for Prohibition. His series of articles helped turn the tide, souring voters on the law by revealing the hypocrisy of the whole thing. Today, Cassiday has a local, D.C. brand of gin named in his honor called Green Hat Gin.

For the rest of us poor souls, we had to rely on a different way of getting our booze, whether it was homegrown moonshine in the countryside or bathtub gin in the cities. One of Washington's illicit liquor shops was in the basement of a candy store, within sight of the Capitol dome. Many even got legal doctors' prescriptions for whiskey, for purely medicinal purposes, I'm sure. But if you wanted a cocktail, where to drink it? The elaborate saloons and hotel bars of the Golden Age were no more. Cocktails went into the shadows and into America's original pop-up bars: the speakeasy.

In D.C. alone, there were 3,000 speakeasies around the city, many more than the number of legal bars before Prohibition. They were in basements and back rooms, behind the trap doors, revolving walls, and sliding windows that we associate with speakeasies today. There was music, and entertainment and tons of cocktails. The only problem was very few of them were any good. There's a reason that today's craft cocktail bars look like speakeasies but talk about *pre*-Prohibition drinks. Drinking during Prohibition for most people was just horrible. The only worse time was the 1970s, which we'll get to later.

If there was one good thing about Prohibition, it was that it democratized drinking, in a way. If we were going to break the law, at least we were all doing it together. Suddenly women were stepping up to the bar in equal numbers as men. Whereas the nineteenth-century saloon that Carrie Nation would take an axe to was a male-only world, the speakeasy welcomed this influx of women. They even catered to it, creating fruity and sweet cocktails that they felt would appeal to a lady's palate. Prohibition also helped blur racial boundaries. The speakeasy was a demimonde where people of all backgrounds, who normally were living in racially segregated cities, could mix. You saw this on D.C.'s U Street corridor, which was nicknamed the Black Broadway. It was a historically African-American part of the city, full of the culture, art, and music that would fuel the Harlem Renaissance. Speakeasies abounded in the jazz clubs along U Street, a place where basically anyone could go and drink and have a pretty damn fine time doing it. Jazz legend and native Washingtonian Duke Ellington remembered playing the clubs along U Street for thirsty patrons, with a gallon of corn whiskey sitting on the piano for the equally thirsty musicians.

Frustrated supporters of Prohibition had a national contest to come up with a name for these flagrant flouters who scoffed at anti-alcohol laws. The winning entry was "scofflaw." We were pretty much all scofflaws.

OVER THERE

While these were dark times for drinking in America, the rest of the world was still enjoying the fruits of our Golden Age. American-style bars thrived in cities like London, Paris, and Rome, and throughout the British empire in places as far away as Singapore and Egypt. The bright young things of the Jazz Age flocked to Europe, where the party was still going strong. F. Scott Fitzgerald, his wife, Zelda, and Ernest Hemingway were some of the most visible members of what became known as the Lost Generation.

In Paris, they might be drinking a Sidecar at the Ritz, or a Monkey Gland at Harry's New York Bar (which was also in Paris, despite the name). Harry's Bar invented the Scofflaw cocktail just a few days after the term was coined back in the States as a playful jab at those who were up in arms about the speakeasies. These are the Prohibition-era cocktails worth drinking. They were creative and used all the fine ingredients available in Europe, from vermouths to sherry to cognac.

The owner of Harry's Bar, Harry McElhone, was a New Yorker from Scotland who left the bar at the Plaza before Prohibition, landed in London, and made his way to Paris. Harry published two important cocktail books during the period, *Harry's ABC of Mixing Cocktails* in 1923 and *Barflies and Cocktails* in 1927, both of which preserved for posterity the pre-Prohibition cocktails he would have been serving in New York, as well as the creative new cocktails proliferating in Europe. Perhaps the nexus of these two worlds were embodied by the Jack Rose cocktail.

The Jack Rose was already a popular drink before Prohibition. It's a simple mix of applejack, lemon or lime juice, and grenadine to create a cocktail with a bright pink hue, although its true origins are a little murkier. Some assumed it was simply named for its color, combining the "jack" of its apple brandy and its rose tint. There's even a famous type of rose called the Jacqueminot Rose that could have been an inspiration. Another legend links the drink to the infamous stool pigeon Jacob Rosenzweig, known as "Bald Jack Rose." His testimony in a sensational 1912 mafia murder trial sent the lieutenant of New York City's Police Department's anti-gambling squad to the electric chair. But the Jack Rose cocktail was in circulation at least a decade before that, and its likely creator was a lot less sinister. David Wondrich points to Jersey City bartender Frank J. May, also nicknamed Jack Rose, who used New Jersey's native spirit to create this popular libation.

Regardless, the Jack Rose gained in popularity during Prohibition, using easily obtained applejack and sweetened with grenadine. And it was just as popular in Europe. Ernest Hemingway has his American expat characters throwing back Jack Roses in a Paris bar in *The Sun Also Rises*. In his book *A Drinkable Feast: A Cocktail Companion to 1920s Paris*, Phil Greene shows how the drink morphed to accommodate European tastes and ingredients, adding in vermouth or subbing out the American applejack for French Calvados. Even Harry McElhone's version uses two types of vermouth, gin, and a little orange juice, bridging both sides of the Atlantic.

In London, British bartender Harry Craddock included the Jack Rose in his famous and beautifully illustrated *Savoy Cocktail Book* in 1930, which is still considered a classic. He was an Englishman by birth, but trained behind the stick in New York at some of the best hotel bars of the Golden Age, including Hoffman House and the Knickerbocker Hotel. It's said that he shook the last legal drink in New York (probably more legend than fact) before setting sail for England the next day and starting work at the Savoy Hotel, which was the location of London's first American bar. The bar would soon become known as the forty-ninth state because of all the Americans it attracted fleeing Prohibition (the real title would actually go to Alaska in 1959).

When Craddock himself arrived, he would have been working under the amazing Ada Coleman, known as Coley by her contemporaries, and as Queen of the Cocktail to posterity. She was the rare woman celebrity bartender back then, cherished both for her mixology and hostess skills. For over twenty years she helped create the reputation of the Savoy's American Bar that Harry took over in 1925. One of Coleman's lasting legacies was the Hanky Panky cocktail, a mix of gin, sweet vermouth, and the bitter Italian digestif Fernet Branca. In English slang, "hanky-panky" meant something like "hocus-pocus," but to the American ear, it would have been a suggestive and enticing drink to order. Regardless, it was a delightful concoction made even more magical by Ada Coleman's sleight of hand behind the bar. During this period, Americans traveling even farther afield could order a perfectly balanced cocktail in Tokyo, or a Singapore Sling (made of gin, Cherry Heering, Bénédictine, lime juice, and bitters) in Singapore's famous Raffles Hotel. But most Americans sought out their cocktails a little closer to home, taking steamers down to Caribbean ports like Jamaica, Trinidad, and especially Cuba. As cocktail expert Jeff "Beachbum" Berry observed, Prohibition was "the kindest thing the U.S. government did for Caribbean tourism" since eliminating yellow fever. Havana became a magnet for Americans with money who wanted to drink in luxury without having to slum it at a speakeasy. A number of skilled bartenders who had been working in the States before Prohibition also set sail for Cuba to oblige them. *Yanqui* tourists would be drinking the El Presidente, a cocktail made with Cuban rum, vermouth, and curaçao, and the Hotel Nacional Special, a mixture featuring rum, apricot brandy, pineapple, and lime juice. Or perhaps they would have gravitated toward a Mary Pickford, a drink named for America's silent film sweetheart, which combined white rum, pineapple juice, grenadine, and maraschino.

Places like Sloppy Joe's in Havana welcomed Americans in droves, and helped reintroduce them to rum in drinks like the Mojito and the Daiquiri. Berry described how the name of this bar became ubiquitous to traveling Americans, was appropriated by stateside speakeasies, and even became the name of a sandwich in a New Jersey deli inspired by the menu at the Cuban original. How's that for culinary heritage? The American-style bar at the restaurant La Florida in Havana (called affectionately Floridita) became known as the "cradle of the Daiquiri," popularizing the drink with visiting Americans. Cuban bartender Constantino Ribalaigua Vert, called the Cocktail King of Cuba, refined the drink with different forms of ice and mixing techniques that would eventually lure the likes of Ernest Hemingway when he returned from Europe. Hemingway is often associated with the Mojito, but there is no evidence that he actually drank them, as Phil Greene writes in his book, *To Have and Have Another: A Hemingway Cocktail Companion*. Instead, Papa loved his Daiquiris, and he wanted them made his way. He got rid of the sugar because of his fear of diabetes, often doubled the ingredients, and preferred the drink with grapefruit juice. His favorite versions were immortalized at Floridita as the "E Heminway *(sic)* Special" and later, when it was doubled, as the Papa Doble. Hemingway himself is immortalized there by a statue of him eternally seated at its bar.

THE HUMMINGBIRD HAS LANDED

The tourism boom in the Caribbean and Europe was dealt a mortal blow by the 1929 stock market crash and the Great Depression that followed. The party "over there" was suddenly over, and much of the Lost Generation wandered back to the States as it became clear that Prohibition's days were numbered. Morris Sheppard, the teetotaler senator who was considered the father of Prohibition, famously commented that the repeal of it had as much chance as "a hummingbird to fly to the planet Mars with the Washington Monument tied to its tail."

But after thirteen tumultuous years, America had had enough of the Noble Experiment. The Great Depression brought a demand for the jobs that the alcohol industry would create, and helped discredit the Republican Party, which had held the White House through practically all of the years of Prohibition. There was a seismic political shift, and politicians no longer feared the once all-powerful Anti-Saloon League and the Women's Christian Temperance Union. Wealthy political activist Pauline Sabin created a counter organization, the Women's Organization for National Prohibition Reform, that helped marshal more than a million women activists to work for repeal (there should be a cocktail in her honor). In 1933, Franklin D. Roosevelt, a lover of Martinis himself, was swept into office along with a Democratic majority on his coattails, and a mandate to repeal the Eighteenth Amendment. By December 5th of that year, the Twenty-First Amendment was ratified. Prohibition was over. Raise a glass to that!

But amid all the joyous celebrations of repeal, the somber truth remained that these thirteen years had extinguished an entire profession. For cocktails, the Lost Generation included an entire class of proud, trained bartenders who had either given up their shakers and spoons or left America entirely. And with them, a rich cultural heritage of cocktails was almost entirely lost. When it came to reclaiming drinking culture, Americans were starting almost from scratch.

SCOFFLAW COCKTAIL

I have always had a love for neologisms. When the perfect word does not exist, make it. That is exactly what Prohibition-era wordsmiths did. Scofflaw is a kind of portmanteau between the words to scoff and law, or to mock the law, and it so perfectly fit the act of drinking without regard for Prohibition's mandates that it stuck. And it didn't take bartenders long to use it as a name for a cocktail. This drink comes to us from Harry's New York Bar, which is actually in Paris, where serving a Scofflaw was a decidedly legal activity. Juicy rye cocktails are usually a little scary, but this one is easy to drink and comes replete with a spirited historical origin. Drink it often in honor of those who did so in the shadows of the law.

COCKTAIL GLASS (5.5-7.5 OZ.)

1 ounce rye whiskey
1 ounce dry vermouth
½ ounce lemon juice
½ ounce grenadine
Dash of orange bitters

Combine all ingredients in a shaker with ice and shake until cold. Strain into chilled cocktail glass. *Makes 1 drink.*

ORANGE BLOSSOM

Even though I include this recipe for posterity's sake, it represents the nadir of cocktail making. Sure, gin and juice has its place (and the eponymous song is very catchy), but it involves no more skill than pouring things from a big container into a smaller one. (I guess that is what all of us bartenders do, technically.) Its simplicity and reliance on two easily obtained ingredients made it a popular drink during Prohibition. It was reportedly a favorite of F. Scott Fitzgerald and his wife, Zelda, before they decamped to Paris with the rest of the Lost Generation in search of better drinking.

COCKTAIL GLASS (5.5-7.5 OZ.)

1 ½ ounces dry gin
1 ½ ounces orange juice

Combine all ingredients in a shaker with ice and shake until cold.
Strain into chilled cocktail glass. *Makes 1 drink.*

3 MILE LIMIT

Once upon a time, three miles off the coast was considered deep in international waters. You could commit murder, launder money, and drink cocktails in sacred peace. Oh, anarchy, my wild ambitions mirror thee! Okay, you really could not do any of that legally, anywhere, apart from drink cocktails. (It was never technically illegal to drink alcohol in the U.S., only to transport, manufacture, or sell it.) But the 3 Mile Limit made its point. You will also see this drink called the Three Miler and Three Miller. These are all the same drinks, but if you want to pretend you need to try all three, I will not stop you.

COCKTAIL GLASS (5.5-7.5 OZ.)

2 ounces brandy
1 ounce rum
Dash of lemon juice
1 barspoon grenadine

Combine all ingredients in a shaker with ice and shake until cold. Strain into chilled cocktail glass. *Makes 1 drink.*

12 MILE LIMIT

These days, twelve miles is the international norm regarding the limits of a nation's sovereignty. And it's a good cause to add rye whiskey to the 3 Mile Limit's mix of rum and brandy. I actually love these two drinks for that very reason. Small details can sometimes completely change a drink, or provide a subtle but significant change, like in this case. Still, they are different and both worth trying. If you plan on actually going out twelve miles, I would suggest batching a bunch up in advance, diluting the batch with water and chilling them in a cooler while you motor out. Cocktails are a far better afternoon refresher than beer and far easier on the seas—and stomach, than straight booze.

COCKTAIL GLASS (5.5-7.5 OZ.)

1 ounce rum
½ ounce brandy
½ ounce rye whiskey
½ ounce lemon juice
½ ounce grenadine
Lemon twist for garnish

Combine all ingredients in a shaker with ice and shake until cold. Strain into chilled cocktail glass and garnish with lemon twist. *Makes 1 drink.*

DECEMBER 5TH
COCKTAIL (ORIGINAL)

Every year in Washington, D.C., the D.C. Craft Bartenders Guild celebrates the repeal of Prohibition by holding a ball. The first one was held in 2008, where I created a cocktail named in honor of Repeal Day, December 5th. This beauty remains one of my favorite concoctions and something way better than you would have drunk during Prohibition.

COCKTAIL GLASS (5.5-7.5 OZ.)

1 ½ ounces ginger liqueur
1 ounces VSOP Cognac
½ ounce lemon juice
Dash of aromatic bitters
Lemon peel for garnish

Combine ingredients in a shaker with ice and shake until cold. Strain into chilled cocktail glass and garnish with lemon peel.

Makes 1 drink.

CHAPTER FIVE

THE FOUND ART OF DRINKING

Moscow Mule
p116

1940s>1960s

By the mid-1940s, two wars had ended: Prohibition's war on drinking and, subsequently, World War II. (There was also the Great Depression, though the common assertion is that liquor is recession- and depression-proof.) The toll these two wars, and our restrained pocket books, had on the drinking habits of Americans was severe. Prohibition decimated the American spirits industry, and foreign libations like sherry, vermouth, and brandy became rare. Rationing during the war further changed the drinking landscape, and America's cocktail Golden Age became a distant memory. Gone were the bartenders who wore diamond stick pins and commanded crowds. Gone were the Blue Blazers and frosted cups. None of the great bartenders of the pre-Prohibition era were still practicing their trade in the United States. As a result of this vacuum, the once-noble art of professional bartending now became a purview of amateurs and hobbyists. No person exemplified this hobbyist more than one David Embury. Embury, an attorney and cocktail enthusiast, announced proudly in his 1948 book, *The Fine Art of Mixing Cocktails*, that:

> Anyone can make good cocktails. The art of mixing drinks is no deep and jealously guarded secret. Nor is it a skill to be acquired only as the result of years of painstaking effort. It can be learned practically overnight.

This is despite the fact that Embury never worked in the spirits or cocktail trade. His book signaled a new age of drinking, where the dilettante ruled. But Embury's book, though full of caustic wit and sometimes overreaching advice, presents a somewhat convincing argument for how to view cocktails.

If Jerry Thomas's drinking bible was the Old Testament, Embury's book was the New. He breaks down cocktails into base, modifier, special flavoring, and coloring agents; two major categories (sour and aromatic); and six basic drinks that all home bartenders should master: the Martini, Manhattan, Old Fashioned, Daiquiri, Sidecar, and Jack Rose. It was a whole new way of looking at the cocktail, designed to help the amateur develop both a taste and an understanding of how to mix drinks.

WHAT, THEN, IS A COCKTAIL?

While we know the cocktail to be a specific invention, Embury encouraged readers to look beyond its principal ingredients and consider its function. For Embury, that function was as an aperitif, an extension of the same idea floated in the 1806 definition when it was referred to as a "stimulating beverage," but Embury greatly expanded the definition to include a bevy of drinks. And in order to fulfill its function, it must possess the following qualities that he lays out in detail in his book:

> It must whet the appetite, not dull it.
> It must stimulate the mind as well as the appetite.
> It must be pleasing to the palate.
> It must be pleasing to the eye.
> It must have sufficient alcoholic flavor to be readily distinguishable from papaya juice, yet must not assault the palate with the force of an atomic bomb.
> Finally (and remember I am speaking now of cocktails only and not of aperitif wines) it must be well iced.

His principal gripe seems to be that cocktails were made with too much juice, cream, and sweetener, and he singles out the Alexander as an example, a cocktail composed of gin, crème de cacao, and cream. A palate can be a subjective thing—I, for example, like papaya juice just fine—but the point is well taken. Balance is key to the cocktail and its function. In order for the cocktail to serve its new, more refined purpose, according to Embury, it must conform closer to his ideals. And he gets quite colorful in prose when he relates exactly what the effect of a cocktail has on guests:

The well-made cocktail is one of the most gracious of drinks. It pleases the senses. The shared delight of those who partake in common of this refreshing nectar breaks the ice of formal reserve. Taut nerves relax; taut muscles relax; tired eyes brighten; tongues loosen; friendships deepen; the whole world becomes a better place in which to live.

Here, here! And by reexamining the cocktail in an easy-to-understand way, he helped reclaim its culinary aspect in a postwar era enamored with mixes and artificial juices and syrups that threatened to make the cocktail unrecognizable.

THE BASE

Embury's system started with the very base, "spirituous liquor of any kind," and he mentions whiskey, gin, rum, and brandy as examples, though he also makes exceptions for fortified wines, citing the classic Vermouth Cocktail and the Bamboo (made with sherry). For Embury, the base must occupy more than 50 percent of the ingredients and, generally, be more than 75 percent of the ingredients. He condones the split base of drinks, using two liquors, but calls three or more "as palatable as a blend of castor oil and gasoline." This is an exaggeration of course, as we'll see in the tiki era that managed to pull off the feat just fine, but it's an exaggeration that the amateur would do well to heed.

THE MODIFYING AGENT

The modifying agent or modifier seems to be the grab bag. This is how you "smooth" out the spirit, and in doing so, move the drink from straight spirit to cocktail. He lists the following categories of ingredients:

A — Aromatics, including the aromatic wines, such as French and Italian vermouth, Dubonnet, Byrrh, etc. bitters of various types—orange, Angostura, Peychaud, Unicum, etc.; and miscellaneous aromatics such as Amer Picon and Fernet-Branca;

B — Fruit juices—orange, lemon, lime, etc.— with or without sugar;

C — Miscellaneous "smoothing" agents—sugar, cream, eggs, etc.

In most cases, he advises caution in using too much modification. The drinks should taste like their base spirit—whiskey cocktails should taste like whiskey; gin cocktails should taste like gin; brandy cocktails should taste like brandy. I compare this to a chef who does not want to drown a good piece of meat in sauce.

SPECIAL FLAVORING AND COLORING AGENTS

This last category he cites includes liqueurs, cordials, and fruit syrups that are added in sparingly. He gives the example of orange juice in the Bronx cocktail. The base is gin, the modifier is sweet vermouth, and the last addition is a little orange juice. (I actually use a lot of O.J.) He issues another warning not to overdo it, to let the spirit be the principal flavor in any cocktail—a sentiment I echo, but one that can also be abused to create cocktails that might as well have been left as straight spirits. Ultimately, despite Embury's insistence that anyone can learn to make cocktails overnight, it's actually a hard line to follow—the art of cocktail making is about dancing with weighted belts.

ROLL YOUR OWN

Though Embury seems to promise six drinks as the Platonic ideals of the cocktail, there are actually no more than two formative cocktails, each done three ways. Embury admits as much with the Daiquiri, Sidecar, and Jack Rose: they're all sours. The Old Fashioned, Manhattan, Martini connection is an argument I've made earlier in this book, and thus, the Old Fashioned is the basis for the other two, with the Manhattan and Martini each essentially composed of spirits plus vermouth and bitters. This means that there are only two principal kinds of cocktails if we get down to brass tacks: sour and aromatic. These two styles of cocktails he elaborates on in a section he calls "Roll Your Own," which helps readers invent their own cocktails informed by the basics.

In Embury's taxonomy, sours are called such because they are patterned after traditional sours, combining a spirit, a citrus juice (usually lemon or lime), and a sweetener. They do not have to be sour tasting per se. The proportions, Embury suggests, are all over the map, and align with each individual's tastes. This is not entirely true in my opinion, as I believe that most sours conform to one of these three categories: equal parts, more sour than sweet, or a Crusta which has just a few dashes of citrus.

Aromatic cocktails, on the other hand, use bitters, aromatized and fortified wines, and liqueurs as the modifiers. An aromatic cocktail is essentially all booze. Embury argues that there are fewer aromatics than sours because, while you can use any fruit juice, you must be more careful when mixing with aromatized and fortified wines, liqueurs, and the like because they employ more botanicals, herbs, and spices. This is total nonsense. Sours, from my perspective, are more linear and limited because they most often employ either lemon or lime. But they can also be plenty hard to get just right—ask any Daiquiri enthusiast.

While Embury's system has a strong internal logic, it's more of a fine art than a science, as his title suggests. He wanted to both refine American palates to appreciate the classics, and democratize the knowledge of how to make them. His book became a bridge across the chasm of Prohibition, blending an appreciation of the past with a "New Frontier" American attitude. The book really does encapsulate the era and a new turn in bartending. While most of his observations feel in touch with today, occasionally you'll hear echoes from Embury of the racism and sexism that made the *Mad Men* era less glamorous and admirable than its style would suggest. This is the part of Embury I cannot endorse. Ultimately, his 1948 book is a Polaroid picture of this moment in time in cocktail culture. (The instant camera became popular that very same year). And in the corner of that picture, maybe still slightly blurry, you can see the image of a new spirit just coming into focus: vodka. It would go on to change the entire picture of American drinking.

A WHOLLY CHARACTERLESS, DILUTE GRAIN ALCOHOL

In David Embury's first edition of *The Fine Art of Mixing Cocktails*, vodka plays just a minor role. He encourages its use as a mixer and calls it "an excellent cocktail base." Within a short time, his tone would change and, by the time the third edition of the book came out a decade later, in 1958, he describes vodka as "… a wholly characterless, dilute grain alcohol that has streaked across the firmament of mixed drinks like Halley's comet," adding: "It is hard to conceive of any worse monstrosity than the Vodka Martini, Vodka-Old Fashioned, or Vodka on the Rocks." Vodka was ascendant and Embury used his curmudgeonly prose to denounce it. Of course, the shot was to no avail. Another decade later, in 1967, it would become the number-one best-selling white spirit in America, beating out Embury's precious gin.

How did this revolution happen, especially considering this was during the rise of the Red Scare and specter of Communism, which theoretically should have deterred Americans from a characteristically Russian spirit? It happened via the trojan horse of cocktails. Specifically, three cocktails contributed to its rise: the Moscow Mule, the Bloody Mary, and the Kangaroo Cocktail (otherwise known as the Vodka Martini).

THE MOSCOW MULE

I remember in the mid-2000s, a rather bro-y gentleman wearing shorts and sandals, with hat turned backwards, coming up to my bar and asking for a Vodka Soda. For better or worse, I had inherited Embury's attitude toward the spirit—a common stance among early craft bartenders—and told him I would make him something better. I stuck with vodka but decided to spice it up and served him a Moscow Mule. For some reason, to me the ginger beer and vodka concoction in a copper mug with mint teeming over the side seemed a hair more respectable. He was sold on it and subsequently ordered three more of these "variations" on the Vodka Soda. I imagine this is how the Moscow Mule caught on to begin with. It is a simple drink masquerading as a craft cocktail, a highball dressed to the nines. Its veneer is what attracts people, but the flavor allows them to wallow in the non-complexity of spicy and sweet.

The most frequent story of the Moscow Mule's invention in the 1940s involves a duo of Americans, John Martin and Jack Morgan. Martin was the owner of G.F. Heublein & Bros., the company that had acquired Smirnoff vodka. Morgan owned the Cock'n Bull on Hollywood's Sunset Strip, which made its own ginger beer. So, they joined forces. This peanut-butter-and-chocolate story was crowned by the copper mugs, which Smirnoff would later manufacture and distribute as a part of a slick marketing campaign for the Smirnoff Mule.

Cocktail writer Eric Felten doesn't buy that story, and sides with the head bartender of the Cock'n Bull, explaining in a 2007 *Wall Sreet Journal* article:

> I find more truth in the story told by Morgan's head bartender, Wes Price, who maintained that the drink was fashioned sometime in 1941 in an effort to offload otherwise unsellable goods.

Turns out that Wes was just trying to get rid of a product no one wanted back then: vodka. This is far more consistent with the recognition of vodka at the time. It was hard to convince a nation of whiskey drinkers to switch to a colorless, odorless spirit with a Russian name (even though it was now being distilled in Connecticut). Embury called the Moscow Mule "merely mediocre," but it caught on with the public, and it was one of two drinks he felt compelled by popular demand to add to his second edition. The other drink was one he called "strictly vile"—the Bloody Mary.

THE BLOODY MARY

I am aghast at what passes for a Bloody Mary these days. For some people, it seems to be merely a delivery system for Tabasco sauce garnished with the vegetable aisle of a supermarket. Adding bacon, hard-boiled eggs, and cheeseburgers to the garnish is just par for the course, though this only heightens my alarm. The true Bloody Mary is so much simpler, and so much more delicious than the monstrosity described above. You may wish to burn your tongue or want food hanging off the side of your drink, but the original has neither feature.

The original recipe, or at least the one that gained the most traction, was from Parisian bartender Fernand "Pete" Petiot. He is often credited with its invention at Harry's New York Bar in Paris in the 1920s, and then with taking it to an actual New York bar—the King Cole Bar at the St. Regis Hotel—where he tried to rechristen it as the Red Snapper. There's a competing claim from American comedian George Jessel, but rather than struggle to figure out the true progenitor, I'm content to say that both claims have some credibility. Yet Petiot is clearly the one who provided the best recipe for our purposes, which is to drink it. He added vodka, tomato juice, Worcestershire sauce, cayenne, salt, pepper, and lemon. Though it has a hint of spice and is sometimes properly garnished with a lemon and a lime, nowhere does his recipe instruct you to dump the proverbial kitchen sink in it. And, speaking of kitchen sinks, perhaps no drink has been more dumped into than the Martini.

THE KANGAROO COCKTAIL

In the 1950s, the Vodka Martini was simply called the Kangaroo. For me, this conveys the true nature of this cocktail: something that is identified with silly animals that hop around in foreign countries. We've already seen how the Martini underwent several iterations in the early twentieth century, and going from sweet to dry is in some ways no more a leap (no pun intended) than going from gin to vodka. Still, this move may have proven a genius marketing ploy if we only knew the genius behind it. It made an otherwise random drink a sophisticated, elegant pour, one that would later become so popular that using the very word "Martini" now conjures a choice—gin or vodka. I will concede this choice, but only if we can admit that a Martini is first and foremost a gin drink.

IT LEAVES YOU BREATHLESS (NOT REALLY)

The vodka invasion of America continued, with the Martini serving as an effective infiltrator. Add to that the Screwdriver and Vodka Collins, and you had an entire repertoire of vodka-based delivery systems—I mean cocktails—to choose from. And then the advertising department got hold of it. Smirnoff devised a very specific campaign, starting in the 1950s and going well into the 1960s, that popularized vodka, and with it, vodka cocktails. It started with a very simple phrase: "It leaves you breathless," implying that the purportedly odorless, colorless, and flavorless beverage could not be detected on your breath when you returned to work after that three-Martini lunch. I detect a whiff of something else, which is anything but odorless. You see, vodka always tastes like something and smells like something. But that did nothing to deter celebrity endorsements—Groucho

Marx, Eartha Kitt, and Woody Allen all joined in promoting Smirnoff. The brand became a sensation and other brands would follow suit, including a deal that Pepsi would make with Russian brand Stolichnaya to become the first Russian vodka sold in the United States. Never mind that the Cold War was getting hotter. America's business is business. Yet it was not just the Russians who were invading; it was our allies as well. The real British invasion came several years before the Beatles.

DOUBLE O SEVEN

Why is it that the guy who comes up to the bar and orders his Vodka Martini "shaken and not stirred," repeating the 1958 James Bond line from *Dr. No*, is never wearing a tuxedo, but always slovenly dressed? When James Bond orders his Martini that way, it makes sense. Here is an iconoclast, dressed the part, but a true individual who bumps gin for a newer, more modern spirit. It fits his entire demeanor. Personally, I think it's a little dated for 2018, but it was a shot across the bow in the 1950s. It makes sense for him. However, the schlub who repeats the line verbatim does not deserve the same level of respect. Oh, fine, ask for your Martini shaken. Just leave James Bond out of it.

Still, it's clear that James Bond's rhetorical stance continues to have an effect on the drinking populace. His repeated requests for shaken Martinis with vodka gave the drink a big boost (and carried it far beyond its Kangaroo days). However, the original 1953 Ian Fleming novel *Casino Royale* has James Bond actually ordering a drink called the Vesper, which he states is:

> Three measures of Gordon's, one of vodka, half a measure of Kina Lillet. Shake it very well until it's ice-cold, then add a large thin slice of lemon peel.

Before you get excited to try the original, I have a few notes. First, it tastes terrible. It is four and a half ounces of alcohol shaken until you cannot taste the alcohol anymore. Second, Kina Lillet is not the same as contemporary Lillet, which is a little sweeter and simpler than its bitter predecessor. If you intend to drink this monstrosity, at least get it right. Try it with a quinquina, an aromatized bitter liqueur. Then enjoy the cold burn.

I want to make a quick disclaimer that though I seem to be attacking the dress of my patrons who order vodka-anything, I really think it is just context. James Bond should order his drink his way. You should order yours your way. The next chapter will show that I am not a snob as we delve into the exotic world of tiki. Here it is absolutely permissible to roll off the beach and order in flip-flops and an Aloha shirt. And to have it shaken (or swizzled) until chillingly cold.

THE BRONX

When I first came across this recipe, it seemed like an odd duck. OJ and gin—aka gin and juice—has never been an appealing combination to me. Throw in two different vermouths and you might as well have told me to put peanut butter on a steak. Yet after trying it, I realized how immensely refreshing and simple a drink it is. It follows drinks like the Cosmopolitan, which have an appeal that is simple, sharp, and pleasurable. Don't think too hard on this drink. It is what it is.

CHILLED COCKTAIL GLASS (5.5-7.5 OZ.)

2 oz. dry gin
½ ounce sweet vermouth
½ ounce dry vermouth
1 ounce orange juice

Combine all ingredients in shaker with ice and shake until cold. Strain into chilled cocktail glass. *Makes 1 drink.*

BLOODY MARY

I have already described the sin of the Bloody Mary as two-fold: too spicy, over garnished. However, I would like to mention one other issue I've seen crop up. For some, the key to a Bloody Mary is canned (or bottled) tomato juice. For a classic Bloody Mary taste, that is absolutely true. However, I would not dismiss fresh tomato juice so easily. I have grabbed ripe tomatoes from the farmers market and squeezed them into the drink with wonderful results. For me, using fresh tomato juice makes a lighter, sweeter drink that highlights the fruit character of the tomato versus the umami. Try it during the height of summer and you will not be disappointed.

HIGHBALL GLASS (12-14 OZ.)

1 ½ ounces vodka
2 dashes Worcestershire sauce
4 dashes Tabasco sauce
Pinch of salt and pepper
¼ ounce lemon juice
4 oz. tomato juice, fresh or canned
Lemon and lime wedges for garnish

Combine ingredients in one shaker and have another empty shaker ready. Mix by rolling (pouring from one shaker to another with no ice). Pour over ice into highball glass. Serve with lemon and lime wedges.

Makes 1 drink.

MOSCOW MULE

The word basic gets bandied around a lot these days, but to a bartender, nothing signals basic more than the Moscow Mule. That does not make it bad, but it does make it a universally acceptable order. Therefore, I recommend this become one of your party drinks of choice when serving a general crowd. If you want to add something unique, try muddling lemongrass or basil in the mug. Those savory but bright notes add a little complexity to the drink and will make you look like a star. A word of caution: people will steal your copper mugs. It is okay to serve this drink in a highball, too.

COPPER MUG (12-14 OZ.)

1 ½ ounces vodka
¼ ounces lime juice
4 ounces ginger beer
Lime wheel for garnish
Basil or lemongrass for garnish (optional)

Build liquid ingredients in a mug filled with ice. Garnish with a lime wheel or basil or lemongrass for a pleasing aromatic character.

Makes 1 drink.

VODKA MARTINI

I think I have already leveled all the vitriol I can at this drink, so let me tell you what I like about it. It is cold. It goes well with seafood. It can be shaken and you are committing no mortal sin. It saves your good vermouth for better things. Olive juice improves it, and nothing else. How's that?

CHILLED COCKTAIL GLASS (5.5 TO 7.5 OUNCES)

2 ½ ounces vodka
¼ ounces dry vermouth
Dash olive juice (optional)
Olive or lemon peel for garnish

Combine all liquid ingredients (including optional dash of olive juice) in a mixing glass or a shaker with ice and stir or shake until very cold. Strain into chilled cocktail glass and garnish with olive or lemon peel.

Makes 1 drink.

THE PHILLY SLING
(ORIGINAL)

The Philly Sling is a sour ostensibly, but has only a small amount of citrus. If you use the right sloe gin, and not the cheap stuff, it should not be too sweet and add a little zing. However, if you prefer richer cocktails, as I do, then the ¼ ounce of simple syrup is essential. I first made this drink for a roving speakeasy bar I created with two friends called Hummingbird to Mars (more on that later). Why is it called the Philly Sling? I hate to admit it, but I named it such because I wanted it to sound like a classic cocktail. The Philly part is a nod to the great, modern-day bartenders that came out of Philadelphia, such as Phoebe Easmon and Christian Gaal.

CHILLED COCKTAIL GLASS (5.5-7.5 OUNCES)

1 ½ ounces applejack
1 ounce sloe gin
½ ounce lemon juice
¼ ounce simple syrup (optional)
Dash of Fee Brother's Whiskey Barrel Bitters
Apple dollar for garnish (see instructions below)

Combine liquid ingredients in a shaker with ice and shake until cold. Strain into chilled cocktail glass. Garnish with apple dollar made by cutting a thin apple slice horizontally through core, then removing core from center of slice with cookie cutter or jigger, and adding to drink.

Makes 1 drink.

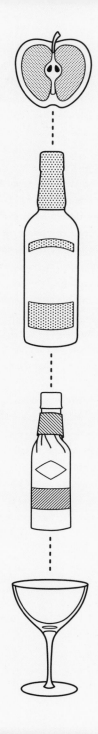

CHAPTER SIX

Mai Tai
p132

TIKI & EXOTIC DRINKS

1930s>1970s

In 1959, Hawaii became America's fiftieth state. While the Union was just officially welcoming the culture of the Pacific islands into its fold, drinkers—as usual— had gotten there first. Americans on the mainland were already sipping cocktails from exotic vessels under thatched roofs that came straight out of a Hawaiian vacation luau. It was a tiki world, and we were just drinking in it.

Of course, it wasn't true Polynesian culture we were imbibing. These were rum-flavored drinks with tropical fruit juices and elaborate garnishes that only hinted at exotic South Pacific beaches. Even the cups themselves morphed into fanciful creations based on tiki gods, the kind that plagued the Brady Bunch family after their Hawaiian vacation. As Americans rediscovered the art of drinking after Prohibition and World War II, they also discovered a sense of the ersatz in their cups. And appropriately enough, these tropical visions of cocktails were dreamed up thousands of miles from their source material, in none other than Hollywood.

The acknowledged founding father of the tiki movement was himself a master of reinvention. Ernest Raymond Beaumont-Gantt was from a New Orleans family that had joined the Texas oil boom. Given a choice between spending his money on college or a trip around the world, he chose the path less traveled (at least by most Americans). He spent his twenties and the 1920s exploring exotic cultures and sampling their libations. He especially fell in love with the South Pacific, but eventually ran out of money, and so he cooled his heels in Los Angeles through the end of Prohibition.

Beaumont-Gantt made a living parking cars (that ubiquitous Los Angeles occupation, even back then) and even dabbled in some bootlegging. But when Prohibition was repealed in 1933, he was ready. He opened up what's considered the world's first tiki bar in Hollywood. Originally called Don's Beachcomber Café, it later became known as Don the Beachcomber, and it was decorated with assorted souvenirs from his wanderings, and served drinks influenced by his years of travel. His thirsty, Depression-era patrons were eager for a colorful escape, and the fanciful setting drew Hollywood stars like Charlie Chaplin, Marlene Dietrich, and Howard Hughes. His motto: "If you can't get to paradise, I'll bring it to you." Gantt even lent his expertise and décor to Hollywood set designers making island-themed movies. Somewhere along the way, he took on the very persona of his bars. Just as Samuel Clemens became Mark Twain, Ernest Gantt became the eponymous Don the Beachcomber, and eventually legally changed his name to Donn Beach.

THE ZOMBIE

This foundational drink was served up by Donn at his bar in 1934, and helped start the tiki revolution. It also created the classic tiki mold—three different types of rum and a mixture of fresh fruit juices, spices, and syrup. The lore says that Donn mixed one up on the fly to reanimate a patron suffering the effects of a hangover. (A lot of cocktail origin stories start this way). More likely, he spent days experimenting with just the right mixtures and proportions. Regardless, the Zombie became a hit, and Donn increased the marketing appeal by limiting drinkers to two per night. Los Angeles drinking culture was taken over by a Zombie apocalypse, with knock-off versions appearing everywhere, no doubt coming from some of Donn's former bartenders who were wooed by competing bars.

Given that popularity, it's no wonder that Donn resorted to taking the labels off his bottles and replacing them with codes, so that even the bartenders didn't know the true ingredients they were pouring and mixing. Still, a version of the Zombie made it to the 1939 World's Fair in New York, ripped off by Hollywood press-agent-turned-club owner Monte Proser. He made the Zombie famous on the East Coast with a pop-up bar at the fair called Monte Proser's Zombie (he was a promoter after all), and then followed it by brazenly opening his own Beachcomber bar in Times Square, touting it as "Home of the Zombie, the World's Most Potent Potion." (Monte would be more famous for opening up the New York club the Copacabana.) It was advertised for its island mystique and for being so supposedly boozy that you couldn't or shouldn't have a third. Naturally, thrill-seeking drinkers couldn't resist, and the Zombie became a nationwide celebrity. Donn did his best to establish paternity for the drink that launched the tiki craze. Of the Zombie, Donn would later proclaim, "I originated and have served this 'thing' since 1934. Anyone that says otherwise is a liar."

Within a few years, the Zombie apocalypse had taken over most of the country. But like Romero movie knock-offs, the later versions rarely matched the quality of the original. The phenomena merited a disdainful mention from David Embury, who observed in *The Fine Art of Mixing Drinks* that no same bar served an identical version. The only thing they had in common was consuming the brains of those who came into contact with them. Embury dismissed the whole mythology behind the drink as simply a marketing ploy to get into the gullets of gullible Americans.

RUM RESURGENT

Embury was onto something. The mystique behind the Zombie and the other exotic drinks that rose in its wake was indeed all a fake. The real secret about tiki is that it wasn't Polynesian at all. There was no such thing as a traditional Polynesian cocktail. The look of tiki is based on some pretty massive cultural appropriation dreamed up in California. But the taste of tiki is Caribbean drinking culture dressed in a hula skirt. It revived the traditional rum punches that were in vogue in America for two centuries, distilled into a tiki glass with a garnish.

And like its forbears, the cocktail and punch, tiki had a basic formula. As tiki expert Jeff "Beachbum" Berry explains, all of the drinks that Donn developed—more than seventy in all—matched the template of traditional Caribbean rum punches, like the Planter's Punch from Jamaica that Donn particularly loved. There is an old rhyme that helped establish the proper ratios—one of sour (lime), two of sweet (sugar), three of strong (rum), and four of weak (water or ice). Donn would play with the ratios and the ingredients, but this was the original blueprint for tiki.

Until Donn Beach came along, rum was suffering under a cloud in America. It had been replaced by whiskey in the affection of Americans during the Golden Age. And Demon Rum had been one of the rallying cries of Prohibition, which shut down all of New England's rum distilleries. A huge molasses explosion in Boston punctuated rum's American story, happening just a day before the Eighteenth Amendment was ratified. It caused a twenty-five-foot tidal wave of molasses, dubbed the Great Molasses Flood, killing 21 and injuring more than 150 in Boston's North End neighborhood. (There's still a plaque to the disaster near the original site, on a low stone wall on Commercial Street across from Copp's Hill Terrace).

During Prohibition, gin became the spirit of choice, although it was most often adulterated, as whiskey was. Rum was the real stuff, because rum runners were able to easily smuggle it into the country. It was cheap, but there wasn't an adoring audience for it. Very few Prohibition-era cocktails featured rum as the star. Americans who could afford a cruise to Cuba or other Caribbean islands were able to sample the good stuff in their Daiquiris. They were attracted to the newer, lighter styles from companies like the Cuban Bacardi, which were completely different in profile than the traditional, dark American rums. When Prohibition was repealed, the very same year that Donn opened his first Beachcomber, there was a backlog of Caribbean rum available on the cheap. Donn, having become an aficionado of all types and flavors of rum, began to experiment with complex combinations in his cocktails, particularly the Zombie. His drinks were exotic, tasty, and affordable. And just like that, rum in America was back from the dead.

THE MAI TAI

When Oakland restaurateur Victor Bergeron made a pilgrimage to Don the Beachcomber in 1937, he became a true believer. His own restaurant, Hinky Dinks, was a barbecue dive with a good cocktail menu. He even had a Zombie, but gave top billing to his own creation of "The Frankenstein," which never seemed to rise to the same level of fame. After spending about a week in Hollywood going to Don the Beachcomber, he returned to Northern California and refashioned the pedestrian Hinky Dinks into a full-fledged Polynesian paradise, even buying some of Donn's artifacts. On the advice of his wife, he changed the name to Trader Vic's to complement the new theme, and the rest is tiki history.

Victor Bergeron was just as adept at reinvention as Ernest Gantt. And just like Gantt, he became better known by the name of his restaurant chain, Trader Vic's. He even invented an adventurous backstory, claiming that his wooden leg was the result of a shark attack, rather than childhood tuberculosis. In reality, he had never left the country until drinking research took him to the Caribbean in the 1930s. He would go on to create a tiki empire that spread across the globe, the crown jewel of which was the creation of the Mai Tai.

Vic claimed 1944 as the birthday of the Mai Tai, when he mixed one for visiting friends from Tahiti. Fine Jamaican rum, Curaçao, the almond-flavored syrup orgeat, lime, and sugar over crushed ice—so good that one of his friends declared it "the best" in Tahitian, a phrase that starts with the word maita'i. Not a bad origin story. Except that maybe it was invented by Donn Beach all the way back in 1933 as a Mai Tai Swizzle, according to Donn's second wife. Or maybe Trader Vic's Mai Tai was based on another one of Donn's drinks that Vic sampled on his first visit to Don the Beachcomber, the Q.B. Cooler. Nevertheless, modern consensus is that Trader Vic's was the better drink.

The Mai Tai went on to replace the Zombie as the very symbol of tiki, and the drink that launched a thousand Hawaiian vacations. And much like the Zombie, it was a drink countless others tried to take credit for. Trader Vic gave credit where it was due for the Zombie, confirming that Donn was the true father of that drink. But of the Mai Tai, Trader Vic declared in the 1972 edition of his *Bartender's Guide*, "Anybody who says I didn't create this drink is a dirty stinker."

CULINARY COCKTAILS

During the Depression, the closest most mainland Americans could get to island culture was a bar like Don the Beachcomber or Trader Vic's. Those who could afford it continued the Prohibition-era practice of visiting the Caribbean on booze cruises. And then came World War II. Suddenly American GIs had their own (mostly harrowing) experiences in the Pacific. But they had fond memories of being stationed in Hawaii, and James Michener's wartime book *Tales of the South Pacific* (later the more famous Broadway play and movie *South Pacific*) helped propel Polynesian culture into the mainstream. This was a trend that both Donn Beach and Victor Bergeron would tap into to build their tiki empires.

Despite his affinity for the South Pacific, Donn Beach ended up in Europe during the war. After an early injury, he was put in charge of R&R sites for soldiers in France and Italy, a fitting job for a barman. When he returned home, he found that his ex-wife and business partner, Sunny Sund, had expanded Don the Beachcomber into a thriving chain. Under the terms of their divorce, Donn wasn't able to use the name to compete nationally. But the United States didn't yet include Hawaii (it was still a territory), and so Donn packed his bags for Waikiki Beach, which was just starting to become a destination. Jet travel became more accessible after the war and so did Hawaii, which became the ultimate American vacation spot. Donn was finally in his true element, and on an ironic mission to remake Hawaii into his own tiki image. He helped revive some traditional aspects of Hawaiian architecture and decoration that had disappeared over years of Americanization of the islands, and melded that with the tiki aesthetic he dreamed up in California. Even the Mai Tai had to be imported to Hawaii, which happened in the 1950s, thanks to Trader Vic.

The more business-minded of the two, Vic was building his restaurant empire throughout the United States. Trader Vic's was not just a bar. It was a culinary experience of high-end dining with exotic fusion food. Going to Trader Vic's in the 1960s and 1970s was considered a serious night on the town. Vic began to attach his restaurants to hotels, going into business with the growing Hilton chain. Along the way, competing tiki restaurants flourished, adding to the mystique with lit torches, decorative waterfalls and volcanoes, island drumbeats, and ceremonial presentations of communal drinks. There were any number of Traders who popped up: Trader Mort's, Trader Eng's, Trader Dick's, Trader Frank's, Trader Bill's, Trader Bob's … you get the idea. Almost all of them vanished into obscurity, except the grocery chain Trader Joe's, which is still doing just fine, thank you.

What set Donn and Vic apart from their countless imitators was that they had created truly culinary cocktails. They used fresh ingredients and juices and very intricate and delicate balances of spirits. Trader Vic revived the use of exotic sweeteners like orgeat, a syrup made from almonds and orange blossom or rose water that had been a staple of several Golden Age cocktails. And they both paired their drinks with food that was pretty exotic for the 1950s. Everyone seemed to have caught island fever, from venerable food critics to President Richard Nixon, who would frequent the Trader

Vic's in the Statler-Hilton Hotel just steps away from the White House, and reportedly loved his Mai Tais (though a former bartender at Trader Vic's, David Chan, claimed that Nixon's favorite drink was the Navy Grog in an interview with *Washington Post* reporter Fritz Hahn). Trader Vic's Mai Tai was featured in the Elvis movie *Blue Hawaii*, with Angela Lansbury as Elvis's mother ordering a constant supply of them. Ironically, the Blue Hawaii was already a tiki cocktail at that point, created by famed Honolulu bartender Harry Yee of the Hilton Hawaiian Village on Waikiki Beach as a drink to showcase blue Curaçao. Kee also popularized those little paper umbrellas, which added a new accessory to tiki.

THE SWIZZLE

Another accessory that was critical to the tiki bartender was the swizzle stick. We're talking about an actual bar tool and not the logo-emblazoned plastic stirrers that are offered in hotels with your Gin and Tonic or coffee. The real swizzle stick is a rarity except in the most authentic cocktail spots, where it's used much like a primitive blender. It dates back to the mid-1800s, when Frederic Tudor popularized ice down in the Caribbean. It's literally a stick from a shrub native to the islands, *Quararibea turbinata*— or more colloquially, the "swizzle stick tree." The end of the swizzle has multiple prongs that act as a blender when you place the stick between the palm of your hands, insert it into an iced drink, and roll it back and forth. This stirs the drink up to a nice, chilly froth while leaving the ingredients at the bottom undisturbed. A drink stirred in this way is called a Swizzle, which is also a pretty delightful part of any Caribbean holiday.

THE SUFFERING BARTENDER

One of the most famous tiki drinks originated not on the shores of the Caribbean or the Pacific, but on the banks of the Nile. Joe Scialom was one of those bartenders from the Old World who would have been at home in the movie *Casablanca*. He held court at the Long Bar in the famous Shepheard's Hotel in Cairo, frequented mostly by British expats. The Suffering Bastard was purportedly a hangover cure he prepared for British officers before they defeated Rommel's forces in Egypt during World War II. Scialom was the son of a pharmacist, which certainly bolstered his medicinal skills. He went on to serve world leaders and kings and most importantly, journalists, who spread his fame and his drink worldwide. The Suffering Bastard was instantly adopted into the tiki fold, although it morphed into a very different drink on Trader Vic's menu—basically a super-charged Mai Tai, which, much like the Zombie, could be both the cause and the cure of a hangover.

The alternate name for Scialom's cocktail in polite society was the Suffering Bar Steward, which could pretty well describe Scialom himself. Despite being a hero to the British, or perhaps because of it, Scialom was imprisoned by former bar patron and Egyptian president Gamal Abdel Nasser, who suspected him of being a spy during the Suez Crisis. Scialom went into exile, where he found a powerful patron in hotel magnate Conrad Hilton. Hilton installed him in his first international hotel, the Caribe Hilton in Puerto Rico. The bar was already recognized as the birthplace of the Piña Colada, a drink that would go on to dethrone the Mai Tai in the public consciousness. In Puerto Rico, Scialom went full tiki, excited about the wealth of fresh juices and ingredients suddenly at his disposal. Hilton next brought him to his new hotel in Havana, where he oversaw the Habana Hilton's bars, and, ironically, the location of the first international Trader Vic's. Even Hemingway attended the opening of that one.

Another revolution forced our suffering bartender to move once again. When Castro took over Cuba, Scialom took his family to New York, where he brought his exotic drinks to the Plaza and the Waldorf-Astoria. He spent much of the rest of his career traveling throughout the world setting up bars for Hilton properties. In the 1970s, he ended up at the celebrated Four Seasons for famed New York restaurateur Joe Baum, and even opened the bar at the new Windows on the World in the World Trade Center. In the end, the suffering bar steward of international fame retired quietly in Florida. He took his last call in 2004, just as tiki and exotic drinks were experiencing their resurgence. His motto, according to a 1950s *Washington Post* profile: "Mix well but shake politics."

PASSING THE TIKI TORCH

Donn Beach and Victor Bergeron were the twin poles of the tiki movement. They both opened their respective bars in California right after the repeal of Prohibition, popularized their brand of exotic drinking culture, evangelized fresh ingredients, and grew their empires throughout the middle of the twentieth century. They both died at the age of eighty-one, a few years apart from each other in the 1980s, the same period when tiki was relegated to the cocktail graveyard. And ironically, they were both given credit for the Mai Tai in their obituaries in the *New York Times*.

They lived long enough to see their cult of tiki go into slow decline, with the grand tiki palaces throughout the country closing down and being erased from the landscape. In 1989, a certain infamous real estate mogul who would become president closed the iconic Trader Vic's bar in the Plaza Hotel, declaring with no sense of irony that it had become "tacky." Luckily, neither Trader Vic nor Donn Beach were alive to bear that indignity.

Tiki stayed in the grave for about a decade, but like a good zombie, it didn't stay dead for long. There were a number of die-hard fans who had been raised on tiki's faded glory, and wanted to restore it back to life. People like Stephen Remsburg, who amassed the largest collection of vintage rums in his home outside New Orleans, and Sven Kirsten, who started documenting the cultural side of the Tiki craze and coined the phrase "Polynesia Pop." And Otto von Stroheim and his wife Baby Doe, who published a tiki zine and formed a fervent community of tiki followers. And Jeff "Beachbum" Berry, who helped uncover the recipes for some of tiki's most important lost cocktails, including the original Zombie.

The complexity of the original tiki drinks had been masked by years of commercialization and imitation. Tiki cocktails were relegated to afterthoughts in Asian restaurants, and made with mixes instead of fresh ingredients. For those who wanted to explore tiki's lost world, there were some guideposts. Trader Vic had published books of recipes and ready-made mixes and syrups, since he saw a market for the do-it-at home drinker. But Donn Beach never revealed most of his recipes. To decipher the Beachcomber drinks, Jeff "Beachbum" Berry became a cocktail archaeologist, combing through period menus and magazine articles, and most importantly, befriending former tiki bartenders. Don the Beachcomber had spawned an elite fraternity of bartenders; there was a whole community of skilled Filipino bartenders whom Donn had hired in Los Angeles for their facility with fruit juices. They kept the recipes written down in little black books, detailing ingredients and proportions.

With these primary sources, Berry painstakingly unearthed the secret ingredients and mixes, and traced the evolution of individual drinks as their recipes had changed over time. Meanwhile, there was a tiki revival happening, one mixed with a bit of mid-century kitsch and hipster irony. But there were just as many who took tiki seriously, and Berry's scholarship was a godsend to a new wave of tiki bars opening in cities like New York, Los Angeles, and Chicago. Improbably, England helped reignite the tiki flame, nurturing these American original drinks much as they had during the drought of Prohibition. Back in the States, a few of the original tiki palaces continued to keep the flame burning, and evangelists like Martin and Rebecca Cate opened up Smuggler's Cove in San Francisco to ensure that tiki had a permanent home. Jeff "Beachbum" Berry followed in the path of Don the Beachcomber himself by opening his own tiki bar, Latitude 29, in New Orleans, the city that had launched Ernest Gantt on his journey a century before.

Tiki has proven itself much more than a passing fad. As Berry says, few fads last for forty years, from the Depression to disco. It was a full-fledged cultural trend and American export that went global. But back home, a generational tidal wave was coming that would sweep away tiki. As we'll see, it was the advent of disco and the 1970s that, once again, almost killed the cocktail entirely.

MAI TAI

This is the most famous of all tiki drinks, and has become basically synonymous with the American tropical vacation. It's rather simple compared to the intricate mixtures of rums and myriad spirits that grace other exotic drinks—consider it tiki's Old Fashioned. Along with the Zombie, it's a foundational tiki drink that Don the Beachcomber and Trader Vic battled over for official parentage. Most give credit to Trader Vic for at least making the better version, and for publishing the recipe that has been passed down for posterity.

DOUBLE ROCKS GLASS (12-14 OZ.)

2 ounces aged rum
¾ ounces lime juice
½ ounce orange Curaçao
¼ ounce orgeat syrup
¼ ounce simple syrup (see page 63)
Orchid flower or lime wheel, and mint sprig for garnish

Combine liquid ingredients in a shaker with ice and shake until cold. Strain into double rocks glass over additional crushed ice. Garnish with orchid or lime wheel and mint sprig. *Makes 1 drink.*

SUFFERING BASTARD

This tiki drink includes bourbon and not an ounce of rum. Maybe that's because it started life in Cairo rather than the Caribbean. Its famous bartender creator, Joe Scialom, intended it as a hangover cure for British troops fighting the Germans in Egypt in 1942. It also doubles as the "Suffering Bar Steward" in more polite company. (I used to pass on the tall tale that the alternate name was a result of mispronunciation by a Scottish bartender in Egypt, but this is the creative license of my profession.) Trader Vic appropriated the name on his menu for a super-strong Mai Tai, and it was eventually served in its own specially-designed tiki mug, in which the traditional tiki face is holding his head in apparent hangover pain. The original drink is far better, and the ginger beer promises a pick-me-up for the eponymous drinker.

DOUBLE ROCKS GLASS (12-14 OZ.)

1 ounce bourbon
1 ounce gin
1/8 ounce lime juice
Dash Angostura bitters
4 ounces ginger beer
Lime wheel and mint sprig for garnish

Combine bourbon, gin, lime juice, and bitters in a shaker with ice, shake until cold, and strain into double rocks glass over fresh ice. Top with ginger beer and garnish with lime wheel and mint.

Makes 1 drink.

FOGCUTTER

This wonderfully boozy drink can both cut through the fog and induce it. According to Jeff "Beachbum" Berry, it's a prime example of Trader Vic's favorite type of drink: using lemon as a sour, orgeat as a sweetener, and mixing rum with other base spirits. A fogcutter is actually a type of diving knife, and the float of sherry cuts through the flavors of this cocktail quite nicely.

DOUBLE ROCKS GLASS (12-14 OZ.)

1 ½ ounces white rum
½ ounces gin
½ ounce brandy
2 ounces orange juice
1 ounce lemon juice
½ ounce orgeat syrup
½ ounce Amontillado sherry
Mint sprig for garnish

Combine all ingredients except sherry and mint sprig in a shaker with ice and shake until cold. Strain over fresh ice in double rocks glass. Float sherry on top and garnish with mint sprig. *Makes 1 drink.*

QUEEN'S PARK SWIZZLE

This traditional swizzle had the seal of approval from Trader Vic himself, who dubbed it the "most delightful form of anesthesia" around. It hails from Trinidad, and was the signature drink of the luxe Queen's Park Hotel in the 1920s. The original recipe borrowed a darker rum from neighboring Guyana, the Caribbean syrup falernum, which tastes of almond and ginger, and a float of Trinidad's most famous export, Angostura bitters. Combined with ice and mint, and you've got a beautiful, multi-colored cocktail to numb any pain you might be feeling.

HIGHBALL GLASS (12-14 OZ.)
WITH A SWIZZLE STICK (SEE PAGE 200)

1 ounce lime juice (from about half a lime)
4 mint sprigs, plus 1 for garnish
1 ounce white rum
¾ ounce overproof rum
½ ounce rich simple syrup (see recipe on page 60)
½ ounce Velvet Falernum
13 dashes of Angostura bitters

Squeeze juice from half a lime, retaining shell. Add four mint sprigs to bottom of highball glass. Fill highball glass halfway with crushed ice, add liquid ingredients, and swizzle. Add lime shell and fill the rest of the way with crushed ice. Swizzle again until glass is frosted. Top with 13 dashes of Angostura bitters and garnish with mint sprig. *Makes 1 drink.*

THE GETAWAY
(ORIGINAL)

The Getaway remains my most popular and instantly successful drink to date. No other drink have I made that was pretty much perfect on the spot—usually I experiment endlessly to find the right combination. I made this when a couple at my bar, the Columbia Room, asked for a drink that tasted like a Daiquiri, but used Cynar, an artichoke Italian liqueur, during an installment of my favorite game: Stump the Bartender (note the sarcasm). Still, I only wanted to please the guest, and so I put this combination together. Once we made it and deemed it a success, I gave naming rights to the guests. I still have no idea why they settled on the Getaway—vacation, car, or movie? I've always called it the Cynar Daiquiri, myself.

COUPE GLASS (5.5-7.5 OZ.)

1 ounce blackstrap rum
1 ounce lemon juice
½ ounce rich simple syrup (see recipe on page 60)
½ ounce Cynar

Combine all ingredients in a shaker with ice and shake until cold. Strain into chilled coupe glass. *Makes 1 drink.*

CHAPTER SEVEN

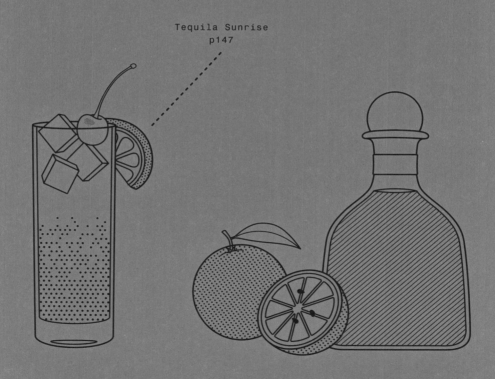

Tequila Sunrise
p147

DRINKING IN THE DARK (AGES)

1970s>1980s

If you're drinking in the dark, it really doesn't matter what your drink looks like. And if you're drinking on a dance floor, you're probably not very concerned with what it tastes like either. This is not the time to be sipping contemplatively on a Manhatttan. It's the time for imbibing with the most efficient alcohol-delivery system possible. In the 1970s, the same went for the bartenders. No meticulous combinations of several different rums and freshly squeezed juices with exotic garnishes. Orange juice from a carton would do just fine. No intricate mixing of quality spirits and vermouths and bitters. How about vodka or tequila and a mixer? And definitely no subtlety of flavors. Maybe just a lot of crème de menthe to make it all go down smoothly. Welcome to the Dark Ages.

In many ways, drinking in the 1970s had a lot in common with that other dark period—Prohibition. Cocktails made with cheap booze, fruit juices, and lots of sweeteners became ascendant. And just like during Prohibition, the real focus for most Americans was just getting drunk, or achieving a similarly altered state. The 1960s counterculture and the shift to mind-altering drugs meant that people didn't want to drink what their parents were drinking, let alone what their grandparents had drunk. Society had changed drastically, and with it so had the cocktails. Fittingly, some Prohibition-era cocktails actually found new life in the 1970s, like the sweet, green-hued Grasshopper, which matched both the color scheme and the taste buds of the era. Other classic cocktails, like the Whiskey Sour, became easier to make with mass-marketed sour mixes, bearing little resemblance to the taste of the originals. (A real Whiskey Sour is a delightful mix of bourbon or rye, fresh lemon juice, and simple syrup, with an optional froth of egg white.) The new drinks that did make it onto menus during the era had names like the Harvey Wallbanger, the Slow Screw, and the Tequila Sunrise. Dark days indeed.

THANK GOD FOR FRIDAYS

I'm looking for a bright spot here, and you know it's desperate times when that glimmer of hope is the chain restaurant T.G.I. Fridays. But stay with me. T.G.I. Fridays started life as a bar on the Upper East Side of New York in the late 1960s. As Robert Simonson describes in his book *A Proper Drink*, it catered to the large population of stewardesses and secretaries who lived in the neighborhood and wanted a welcoming place to go out. The owner, Alan Stillman, geared everything from the décor to the drinks to what he thought would attract women, and consequently men. In effect, it was the first singles bar. Another name for it was the "fern bar"—an allusion to the decorative ferns that made it feel nonthreatening and slightly upscale, along with the faux–fancy Tiffany lamps. T.G.I. Fridays helped start a trend that got young people off the disco floor and back into a traditional bar setting, ordering cocktails.

Today when we think of drinks at T.G.I. Fridays, we think of Mudslides and frozen strawberry Daiquiris. But back in the day, Fridays pioneered a pretty expansive bar program. As Simonson describes, it elevated the bartender to top status and required rigorous training and the memorization of more than 400 recipes. Freshly squeezed juices and fresh mixes were prepared daily. I wouldn't say these were all cocktails at their finest—we're talking a lot of Lemon Drops and Long Island Iced Teas— but as T.G.I. Fridays grew and spawned other imitators, it helped create both a role and set of conduct for professional bartenders again.

SOUR MIX

One of the things that helped bars like T.G.I Fridays crank out cocktails for the masses was the use of sour mix. Powdered beverages then were not viewed with the total scorn we have for them today. In the 1970s, instant powdered beverages had taken a foothold all over the cultural landscape. By the time I was born in 1974, my parents were mixing instant coffee, instant ice tea, and an instant orange drink that fell flat on sales at first but would later gain prominence for making it to the moon and back: Tang.

It is important to note that sour mix itself had existed long before the high-fructose, colored variation arrived on the scene. But these offenders became part and parcel of cocktail culture in the Dark Ages, spawning non-powdered, sweet variations as well.

The turn toward the worst versions was ultimately done because they were cheap to make, cheap to buy, and saved a lot of time behind the bar. Later on, opposition to sour mix would become a flag that craft bartenders hoisted in their war against bad tasting, chemical-laden cocktails. But this ingredient that would sour the craft rose to absolute dominance while the Bay City Rollers blared from the speakers and the bottom of their pants widened. One more reason to blame the '70s.

SEX ON THE BEACH, SCHNAPPS MADE FROM PEACH

As disco morphed into Duran Duran, the drinks went with them. Consider the cocktails of that era like a typical 1980s tune: it might have nonsense lyrics and shallow substance, but it had style. Music then didn't speak to our souls—it spoke to our feet on the dance floor. As a child of the 1980s, when I think about the decade, I think shoulder pads, Reaganomics, the rebirth of punk music, and V-shaped glassware—the ubiquitous martini glass that housed any manner of "Martini." I also think about blue: blue drinks were rampant. But carefully crafted cocktails by skilled artisans was not in my generational vocabulary. What I knew of cocktails (in fairness, I was not yet of the drinking age) was one phrase that summed up the era: grody to the max. They were sickly sweet with tongue-in-cheek names that prevented any serious drinker from taking them seriously. It was also an era of shooters: Kamikaze (equal parts vodka, triple sec, and lime juice), Slippery Nipple (Sambuca, Bailey's Irish Cream, grenadine), and, of course, Jell-O shots.

But one of the defining moments for cocktails in the 1980s was the arrival of a new type of peach liquor on the scene. This had nothing to do with traditional peach brandy, which was one of our earliest and most fruitful American spirits. No, the time for carefully made peach firewater was past. We are talking about another animal altogether, one that has delighted and amazed underage drinkers for decades now: Peach Schnapps, the ultimate party animal.

DeKuyper Peachtree Schnapps was developed by the company National Distillers in response to flagging sales of spirits nationwide. And the company helpfully provided a new cocktail suggestion to go with it. Just as the Moscow Mule was the vehicle for vodka twenty years earlier, the Trojan Horse for peach schnapps was called a Fuzzy Navel, which added vodka and orange juice. Soon peach schnapps was the fastest-growing spirit in the country, and we had a whole new wave of sweet, juice-based cocktails.

Perhaps the apotheosis of this trend was the Sex on the Beach. It combined peach schnapps, vodka, cranberry juice, and orange juice, with no discernible taste of spirits whatsoever. Legend has that it was born on the beaches of Fort Lauderdale in 1987 during a Spring Break competition to devise a way to sell the most peach schnapps. That seems fitting. New cocktails in this era were mostly driven by liquor companies' creative attempts to market and sell their product. The beating that classic cocktails had taken from Prohibition onward—first with bartending being made illegal then subsequently with amateurism and drug culture—was evident. All of this had created a vacuum, and during this decade, consumerism would overtake counterculture. Perhaps nothing publicized that takeover more than the 1988 movie *Cocktail*. One of its most memorable scenes involved a soliloquy delivered atop a bar by Tom Cruise as the last barman poet, singing the praises of "the Sex on the Beach, the schnapps made of peach." Hold on to your drinks, folks—it's about to get bumpy.

COCKTAILS AND DREAMS

Cocktail, for those who have not seen it, is a movie starring Cruise as Brian Flanagan, an ambitious, bottle-flipping, womanizing young bartender. He rises to New York bartending fame alongside his partner, Doug Coughlin, played by Bryan Brown. In the movie, Cruise's character stands up and recites his aforementioned poetry to the cheers of adoring bar fans, learns drinks on the job, and perfects his flair routine, which includes tossing bottles back and forth with his partner. He is unstudied, brash, and arrogant. When we think of the instructions set by Harry Johnson in his 1882 *Bartenders' Manual* that bartenders should be polite, attentive, bright, and cheerful, answering all questions posed, we can see that one hundred years had indeed changed the game. (Though Johnson did try a bit of flair by pouring six cocktails at a time and letting the liquid cascade down pyramid-stacked glasses. And even Jerry Thomas had the Blue Blazer trick up his sleeve.)

Despite our eye rolling today, *Cocktail* inspired more than a few bartenders to the profession. Yet, before it became a flashy 1980s movie, it was a pretty searing, semi-autobiographical novel by New York bartender Heywood Gould. His book chronicled the life behind the stick during the 1970s and early 1980s: long hours, frustrated dreams, and pervasive substance abuse. I interviewed Gould on the occasion of the twenty-fifth anniversary of the movie, and he described the two types of bartenders he encountered during the Dark Ages: The Aristocrats of the Working Class and the Lost Talent. The Aristocrats often came from bartending families and worked at the better hotels or held court at the neighborhood bar, which came with its own kind of prestige. The Lost Talents were like an updated version of the 1920s Lost Generation—frustrated writers or artists or musicians who, like Heywood, were usually biding their time until they hit it big in their desired professions.

And then there were the bartenders who were the inspiration for his character Doug Coughlin, who were forever toiling "across the bar from people they wanted to be, but couldn't make that three-foot jump to join them on the other side. They schemed and dreamed and worshipped success and never got it." He called these bartenders the "hustlers," as opposed to the "workers" who kept the profession humming along. At the end of the movie (spoiler alert), Cruise's character succeeds in opening his dream bar, called Cocktails and Dreams. Gould found his own success as a novelist and screenwriter, and reflected on the change that happened among bartenders within a decade of the movie's release: "Bartending is a profession now, not a job you took until (hopefully) you made it in your art. It was all male [and] now it's half female, although the female bartenders have the same prestige and total authority. Bartenders are like celebrity chefs now. It's a new world."

And yet there had been a bit of distance to travel from there to here. The movie's depiction of bartenders was all style, no substance. And while Gould wrote the screenplay for *Cocktail,* it was drastically different in tone from his book. It had morphed into a slicker affair once Disney took over production and Tom Cruise was cast as the lead. They also added in the acrobatic bartending style called flair to liven up the action. A T.G.I. Friday's bartender, John Bandy, was brought in to train stars Cruise and Brown, and the location of the first bar appearing in the movie was none other than the original T.G.I. Friday's on the Upper East Side. Gould said that the changes in tone—this is the movie soundtrack that brought us the Beach Boys' "Kokomo" and Bobby McFerrin's "Don't Worry, Be Happy"—led to scathing critical reviews that were so bad Gould took to his bed "like a Victorian heroine with the vapors." And for bartenders who had considered the source novel as their Bible, they felt the movie was a betrayal. Even his friends complained to him: "People keep coming up and demanding we juggle bottles like Tom Cruise. Thanks a lot, asshole!"

Still, the movie put cocktails front and center in the public consciousness again, proving that even in the Dark Ages, there were glimmers of hope. We were starting to rebuild the spaces where both men and women could drink cocktails, and we were slowly refilling the depleted ranks of the professional bartender. What we were missing were the recipes and the ingredients that gave the Golden Age its luster. But there was one New York bartender who had thus far toiled in obscurity, but who would help usher in the rebirth of the cocktail. He was one of Gould's "worker" bartenders, but his impact would be so great that he would earn the title "King Cocktail." His name was Dale DeGroff, and he would succeed in reclaiming more than 200 years of our lost drinking history and put us on the road to a cocktail renaissance that we're enjoying to this day.

HARVEY WALLBANGER

Galliano is one of those products that is indispensable in a bar, if only for three very specific reasons. First, its tall, slender bottle shape helps with the measurement of back-bar shelving. Second, its size and thin, tapered neck makes it a handy weapon against would be assailants. And third, it can make a Harvey Wallbanger. There is absolutely no other reason to carry this product. How often do bartenders make Harvey Wallbangers? Almost never, but when that one person orders it and you have Galliano, and a little bit of the now-antiquated knowledge of how to make one, it is the same feeling you get after buying a cup of coffee for someone or letting a driver into your lane—you have made one person's life better in a small, generous way.

HIGHBALL GLASS (12-14 OZ.)

1 ½ ounces vodka
4 ounces orange juice
¾ ounce Galliano liqueur
Orange slice for garnish

Build vodka and orange juice in highball glass with ice. Float Galliano on top. Garnish with orange slice. *Makes 1 drink.*

TEQUILA SUNRISE

The original Tequila Sunrise is a poolside cooler made without orange juice or grenadine, purportedly created in the 1930s to combat the Arizona heat at the Biltmore Hotel. Yet the real progenitors of the cocktail—or at least the ones who popularized it—are The Rolling Stones. Bobby Lozoff, who has a counterclaim to having created the Tequila Sunrise at the Trident in Sausalito, California, served it to The Rolling Stones in place of a Margarita in 1972. They would name their tour that year in support of Exile on Main Street the "Tequila Sunrise Tour." Or what Keith Richards called the "Cocaine and Tequila Sunrise Tour."

HIGHBALL GLASS (12-14 OZ.)

1 ½ ounces silver tequila
4 ounces orange juice
Dash of grenadine
Orange slice and cherry for garnish

Build tequila and orange juice in highball glass with ice. Add grenadine and jiggle drink with a bar spoon until the layers settle (the effect should look like a sunrise). Garnish with orange slice and cherry.

Makes 1 drink.

SLOW SCREW

Here is that OJ and booze category once again and, no,
I have not changed my mind. Do not make this drink,
unless you truly want to channel the era, and you have
to find another use for your bottle of sloe gin. The Slow
Screw is based off the Screwdriver, but adding sloe
gin to the mix. Get it? It spawned a whole category of
drinks using similar puns. The Slow Screw Against the
Wall (with Galliano, also used in a Harvey Wallbanger),
Slow Screw on the Beach (based on a Sex on the Beach
with Peach Schnapps) and a Slow Comfortable Screw
Up Against the Wall (throw in some Southern Comfort).
The whole thing is despicable. Yet, I do find it kind of
entertaining. So there is that.

HIGHBALL GLASS (12-14 OZ.)

1 ounce vodka
1 ounce sloe gin
3 ounce orange juice
Orange slice for garnish

Combine all ingredients in a shaker with ice and shake until cold.
Strain over fresh ice in highball glass. Garnish with orange slice.

Makes 1 drink.

WHITE RUSSIAN

The White Russian is based off of the Black Russian,
which is vodka and Kahlua. Not a bad drink, but nothing
special either. But once you've seen *The Big Lebowski*,
there is no way you can forget The Dude and his version
with non-fat, powdered dairy creamer. Don't do it,
though. Heavy cream is far better. Either way, save this
drink for after dinner. It is the furthest thing from an
aperitif or a food-friendly drink.

DOUBLE ROCKS GLASS (12-14 OZ.)

1 ounce vodka
1 ounce Kahlua liqueur
1 ounce heavy cream

Build vodka and Kahlua in double rocks glass with ice. Pour cream over,
stir, and serve. *Makes 1 drink.*

STAY OFF THE GRASS (ORIGINAL)

The hosts of the radio show the *Dinner Party Download*, Brendan and Rico, asked me to create a cocktail for their segment "A History Lesson...with Booze." Naturally, I complied, only to find out that the history period they chose was one of the worst for cocktails ever: the 1970s. They wanted me to make a cocktail encapsulating the history of Studio 54 and the creation of the song "Le Freak." So, I did. I started with a Grasshopper as the base, which is a great old cocktail that found its way into 1970s drinking culture. It tastes of ice cream and mint—not bad. My version adds a little more depth and comes with a warning in its title.

CHILLED COCKTAIL GLASS (5.5-7.5 OZ.)

1 ounce Brandy de Jerez
¾ ounce heavy cream
¾ ounce cream sherry
½ ounce crème de menthe
½ ounce creme de cacao
Half a teaspoon of cold brewed coffee
1 sprig of chocolate mint for garnish

Combine liquid ingredients in a shaker with ice and shake until cold. Strain into chilled cocktail glass. Garnish with chocolate mint sprig.

Makes 1 drink.

CHAPTER EIGHT

Cosmopolitan
p162

REBIRTH OF THE COCKTAIL

1980s>1990s

I still remember the moment that I became aware—just vaguely—of classic cocktails. It was 2001, and I worked at a bar in the Adams Morgan neighborhood of Washington, D.C., called Rocky's Cafe. Don Lawson, a bartender at the restaurant next door, Cashion's Eat Place, sat down and, instead of his nightly order of Vodka Soda, he ordered a Sazerac. Sazerac? He might as well have said Xanadu. I had no idea what he was talking about. You see, I had lied my way into the job with zero skills (apart from bullshitting) and to that point the majority of "cocktails" I had made had the ingredients in their titles: Vodka Soda, Jack & Coke, Gin & Tonic. The best I could do was an absurd version of Rum Punch. (When I was interviewed for the job, Rocky asked me if I knew how to make a Rum Punch. I said yes without ever having made a cocktail professionally before in my life. I grabbed all the rums on the rail—gold, dark, white—all the fruit juices and sour mix, and garnished it with all the fruit—lime, lemon, pineapple, and cherries. Close enough.)

Don explained the Sazerac was an old cocktail he learned while working in New Orleans and rattled off the ingredients: rye whiskey, absinthe, sugar, and bitters. Of those ingredients, we only had sugar. Rye was hard to come by, and absinthe was still technically illegal. So, the prospect of making this cocktail was slim indeed. We didn't even have a cocktail spoon—and this cocktail is stirred. Such was the state of many bars circa 2000.

My next job was at a restaurant in Washington called Palena that was much more cocktail focused. They had barspoons, a Vodka Espresso (aka the Espresso Martini) on the menu, and an array of amari from Italy. They also had a beautiful poured concrete bar that looked almost like marble and lighted mirror boxes that displayed the spirits. There were large, cozy cloth stools with rolling backs. I was smitten. And, by then, I had this idea that I would revive classic cocktails, having just read William Grimes's seminal 1993 book, *Straight Up or on the Rocks*. And now that I was working in a proper cocktail bar, I especially wanted to bring the Sazerac back to glory. The first trick would be to find rye whiskey and Peychaud's Bitters. I also knew of an absinthe substitute called Herbsaint available in New Orleans. A friend was traveling to New Orleans, so I begged her to pick up a bottle for me and she did.

Then this happened: I succeeded in replicating a Sazerac. In fact, the chef of Palena, who had an incredible palate, told me he could sip the drink all night long—an amazing compliment, especially considering he gave them so rarely. But I would not be the one to bring back classic cocktails. Unbeknownst to me, that ship had set sail long ago. There was already a renaissance underway, the roots of which began in the 1980s in New York City by a man we rightfully call King Cocktail, Dale DeGroff.

KING COCKTAIL

I think when most people make Dale a drink for the first time, their hands tremble just a little. Mine definitely did. I was being tested at a bar course called the B.A.R. 5-Day Program. B.A.R. stands for Beverage Alcohol Resource, a course taught by leaders in the bar and spirits industry, including DeGroff, Doug Frost, Steve Olson, David Wondrich, F. Paul Pacult, and Andy Seymour. During the test, I accidentally made a Margarita with a sugar rim instead of salt. Needless to say, I did not pass (though I would later retake the test and finally did). Dale was jovial about the whole thing. I am sure it's not the first bad cocktail he had received in his life.

Without Dale DeGroff, the renaissance that transpired wouldn't have had its leader, and may not have happened at all. There were certainly many great bartenders that existed, even during the darkest days. We talk about the 1970s and 1980s as the Dark Ages, but we also forget that during the actual Dark Ages, there were brilliant philosophers and alchemists who would plant the seeds of a revolution in thought, acting as flickers of light in the darkness. Dale was that and more for the cocktail movement. The story he tells is that he was a young actor in New York and started working with Joe Baum. Baum was a legendary New York restaurateur (the same one who had brought famed bartender Joe Scialom to the Four Seasons and Windows on the World), and wanted to revive the Rainbow Room. But he needed a bartender with all the class and sophistication of the bartenders of the Golden Age. Dale had worked in New York for Baum and then left for a stint in Los Angeles at the Hotel Bel-Air. Baum offered Dale this new gig, and when Dale returned to New York, Baum told him to go out and get a copy of Jerry Thomas's 1862 bar guide. He forgot to tell him it was out of print.

Dale complied, and despite the difficulties in tracking a copy down, worked diligently to study and prepare cocktails that had not been seen for almost one hundred years. Soon, smashes and sours were gracing the tables of the refurbished New York night den, and what Dale thought would be a slow burn was an instant success. He flamed orange peels, used large ice, traded in sour mix for fresh juice, dropped the soda gun—and the renaissance was underfoot. For twelve years, Dale was the Rainbow Room's "master mixologist," a title that had not been used since before Prohibition. Though he traded in the classics, one cocktail would come to dominate the next decade and become the unwitting enemy and savior of the cocktail movement—the Cosmopolitan.

THE COSMOPOLITAN

For a time during the late 1990s and 2000s, cocktail programs had one distinguishing cocktail that was an absolute must: the Cosmopolitan, or Cosmo as it is sometimes called. The original spawned countless variations during the era, often featuring tweaks on the ingredients, using infused vodkas, and sometimes being named for the establishment or person who invented them. The calling card though was a light pink, sour drink, and that card was called often.

The rise of the Cosmo began in the 1980s with the rise of citrus vodka, one of the first of a new category of flavored vodkas. Dale is often credited with the Cosmo's invention, though he himself says that he only standardized the recipe. Writer Robert Simonson suggests the likely author of the drink is Toby Cecchini, a New York bartender who ran the famous Passerby bar known for cocktails and its disco floor. Bartender and author Gaz Regan also credits Cheryl Cook, who was serving them in South Beach, Miami. And as for popularizing them, it certainly didn't hurt when Madonna was photographed drinking one of Dale's Cosmos in the Rainbow Room.

The Cosmopolitan was much ordered and much maligned during the decade that followed. The color, the name, its popularity, the person who was likely to order it to imitate *Sex and the City*—all contributed to its infamy. But the bones of the cocktail are good. In fact, Chris McMillian, a New Orleans bartender and co-founder of the Museum of the American Cocktail with Dale DeGroff, argues that it is easy to see the lineage of the drink going back to the crusta, a proto-sour found in Jerry Thomas's original bar manual. And, in fact, it deserves the same line in history as the Daiquiri. Maybe. It also has many similarities with the Kamikaze shooter. And it definitely relies on an ingredient that would gain as much traction in the 1980s and 1990s as it had in the 1950s and 1960s—vodka. The only difference was that this time, the vodka had flavor.

THE RISE OF FLAVORED VODKA (AND INFUSIONS)

Let's start by saying flavored vodka is a scourge. Whether it is whipped cream flavored or electricity flavored (both exist), it has become a category that plays to the lowest common denominator: all kitsch and flash with very little quality. Sometimes there is a breakthrough flavored vodka that is well made and well liked, but that is the outlier. More often it is alcohol that, unfortunately, caters to children: sweet, artificial, and artfully packaged.

The very first of its kind actually predates the category as a whole. Russians had infused vodka with fruits and herbs for a very long time. In Poland, Zubrowka added bison grass for a sweet herbal and vanilla-like taste. And aquavit, for all intents and purposes, is flavored vodka. Hell, even gin is a kind of flavored vodka, as a neutral spirit that's infused with botanicals. Those, of course, are not the flavored vodkas I mean. The category of flavored vodka I'm talking about is something altogether different. It started in 1986 with Absolut Peppar, a pepper-infused spirit ostensibly intended for Bloody Marys, but has been since used in an array of drinks. Shortly after, citrus vodka became popular (especially with Cosmopolitans). Something interesting happened though. Where commercially flavored vodkas fed an appetite for cheap infusions, around it a culture of infusions grew. In fact, I would say that most of us who were disappointed in what passed for flavored vodka took matters into our own hands. That is why, in part, the beginnings of the rebirth of the cocktail during this period involved a healthy dose of infused spirits.

THE FIRST FOLLOWERS

While Dale was slinging Cosmos and flavored vodkas were proliferating, something even bigger was brewing. We can't rightfully give Dale all the credit for reviving classic cocktails any more than we can say the match that strikes a pile of kindling is alone responsible for the fire. The kindling matters too. It was those who followed Dale's example that produced the groundswell that would become the classic cocktail renaissance, revolution, or whatever you want to call it. Many of the first wave of bartenders to introduce methods and ideas from classic cocktails were directly influenced by Dale DeGroff, especially Tony Abou-Ganim, Audrey Saunders, and Julie Reiner to name a few. These bartenders would not only refine and improve the craft, but also inaugurate a second wave of bartenders after them that would become today's icons of the bar world. And while Dale deserves credit on this side of the pond, London bartenders and their cocktail scene at the time are another important story altogether.

THE OTHER KING OF COCKTAILS

While America is not used to crowning kings, in London, another King Cocktail comfortably reigned. His name was Dick Bradsell, and he is heralded as the man who brought back classic cocktails in London. Besides the Cosmo, perhaps the cocktail I made the most of in the beginning of my career was the Vodka Espresso (aka the Espresso Martini). That drink was invented by Dick in London the 1980s. Working at bars such as Fred's, Zanzibar, Colony Room, and his namesake, Dick's Bar at the Atlantic Bar and Grill (where he worked for a total of six months), he was known for being prolific in creating cocktails, being a friend to all, and for establishing the basics of the craft.

He was also a devotee of David Embury and took particular care with the Daiquiri. Writing for *Difford's Guide*, a London-based drinks website, Dick relayed how influenced he was by Embury's account of Constantino

Ribalaigua Vert, Cuba's renowned master of the Daiquiri, fixing a Daiquiri and how it was a dream to visit Cuba. The Daiquiri became his test for excellence in bartending. Dick was known for a number of cocktails, but besides the Vodka Espresso, the one he is most famous for was the Bramble, a simple concoction of dry gin, lemon, simple syrup, and crème de mûre (blackberry liqueur). Notably, all of his cocktails featured fresh juices, which was something rare in those dark days.

THE DEATH OF SOUR MIX

If I was to name one ingredient that become the flash point of the classic cocktail movement, it would be sour mix. If you have never tried sour mix, you have been spared the indignity of this watery, Gatorade-like lemonade. Good for you. It was sometimes made from a powder and often bought in bulk, but all of it was total garbage. Perhaps its origin was sound: you take lemon and lime, sweeten it, and maybe add some egg whites. It was an easy stand-in for citrus in drinks such as the Whiskey Sour—not that I endorse this practice at all. Because really, how hard is it to squeeze a fresh lemon or lime?

Bartenders like Dale DeGroff, Dick Bradsell, and their protégés instituted many changes that would revolutionize the bar world, but none more profound than squeezing fresh juice. In fact, it is so simple that it is easy now to overlook how exceptional this idea was at the time. Want a Daiquiri? Before DeGroff and Bradsell, it would be just rum and sour mix (if it wasn't preblended in a machine). Want a Vodka Sour? Add vodka and sour mix, and voilà—you've got a drink that tasted just like sour mix, i.e., disgusting. The uproar that the fresh juice initiative caused was divisive. Bartenders would scream and swear that squeezing juice was the greatest evil to have befallen the profession. It takes too long to squeeze. It does not last long enough. It costs too much. Bartenders took their stand on both sides. Some, such as the leaders of the craft movement, for fresh juice; others, the ones who would eventually be cast aside, for the mix.

BOND REDUX

There was one cocktail in particular that was a dreaded order in those early days because of its reliance on fresh, muddled ingredients whose preparation took up bartenders' valuable time and resources: the Mojito. The first punch in this fight happened in the 1990s and early 2000s, when the charming Buena Vista Social Club, a musical ensemble playing classic Cuban music from the 1940s and 1950s, revived an interest in all things Cuban, including the Mojito. The second punch was in 2002, when the Bond film *Die Another Day* was released with a new Bond, Pierce Brosnan, a new Bond girl, Halle Berry (the best one, in my opinion), and a new drink: on a beach in Cuba, Bond orders a Mojito.

The Mojito was suddenly in hot demand, and bartenders were not having it. Everything about their resistance smacked of those lazy days when bartenders poured shots, beers, and if any cocktail, a Manhattan. First, a Mojito is something you have to have fresh ingredients for—you need both mint and limes. Second, you have to muddle it. Muddling, oh the indignity! Bartenders were forced to twist a stick repeatedly to release the flavor of the mint. You also had to have sugar handy, and there was a good chance if you made one you would make a dozen more once somebody saw it. You would also likely be covered in sugar and mint by the night's end. I know it sounds ridiculous now, but the Mojito represented a truly pitched battle between guests and bartenders. Of course, we know who won.

THE RISE OF THE COCKTAIL NERD

When I was young, you did not want to be a nerd. It was not a good thing as it is today, celebrated in TED Talks, Comic Cons, and by glorified leaders of tech companies. Being a nerd meant you were physically weaker, even if mentally stronger, and forced to submit to every indignity bestowed upon you by the cool kids, jocks, and, well, anyone else. You were the lowest on the food chain and it felt sad. I think of *Revenge of the Nerds*, a movie that came out in the mid-1980s, about a tortured band of nerds who gathered together under the fraternity Lambda Lambda Lambda to fight against the jocks until through sheer tenacity and a little bit of genius, they prevailed. Still, they were nerds.

Three things would change that in my mind and allow myself to proudly call myself a nerd. First, with the rise of the internet and subcultures, every nerd found a home. Second, the nerds who both made the internet and proliferated its sites, got really rich and now seemed much cooler than they had before. And finally, nerds (and geeks) embraced cocktail culture. They set up the first craft cocktail chat rooms, message boards, internet sites, blogs, and more. What had been a fractured group of people with an interest in better drinks became a collective force united under the banner of classic cocktails. What started as a few leaders and their nascent followers became a full-fledged people's revolution—cocktails were ascendant again.

One of the names that deserves mention in those early days is Ted Haigh. Through his cocktail persona Dr. Cocktail (in real life he works as a graphic designer in Hollywood), he led the AOL chat rooms as the cocktail maven, unearthing old recipes, stories, and, famously, old bottles of booze. By his own admission, he has a lot of old bottles. He would later found the now defunct CocktailDB.com: The Internet Cocktail Database, which became the single best source for classic cocktail recipes.

However, for me, the sign that nerds now ruled the cocktail scene was DrinkBoy.com, created by Microsoft technology evangelist Robert Hess. Finding his website, which he started in 1998, was like finding a lost treasure map. There were articles on how to make bitters, finer debates about the history and technique behind cocktails, and news from the cocktailsphere. My budding interest in classic cocktails became a full-blown obsession, and I scoured the site for any piece of information I could find. The cocktail renaissance, now in full effect, had in place its leaders, first followers, propaganda ministry, and, in me, a committed soldier.

COSMOPOLITAN

How strange it seems now to enter this drink into the annals of classic cocktail history, but guess what? It belongs here. Not only is it an essential part of the rebirth of cocktail culture, but when made properly, it really does taste pretty good. Sure, it's not a Sazerac, complex and layered. That I will concede, but it does the trick and looks pretty doing it. So, congratulations, Cosmo, you made it after all.

COCKTAIL GLASS (5.5-7.5 OZ.)

1 ½ ounce citrus vodka
½ ounce Triple Sec
1 ounce cranberry juice
¼ ounce lime juice
Orange peel for garnish

Combine liquid ingredients in a shaker with ice and shake until cold. Strain into chilled cocktail glass. Garnish with flamed orange peel.*

Makes 1 drink.

*The orange peel can be flamed by expressing the oils from the exocarp (outside layer) of the peel over a match or lighter held over the glass to ignite the oils. There will be a flare-up of flame, so be careful to not burn your hand.

CABLE CAR

This drink by the talented and jovial bartender Tony Abou-Ganim makes an obvious reference to the Sidecar, another classic that came back in the 1990s. Originally, Sidecars didn't have sugar rims. That was the Crusta, an elaborate cocktail that debuted in New Orleans in the 1850s. The Crusta was out of style by the turn of the twentieth century, and was eventually conflated with the very similar Sidecar. It became popular in Europe during Prohibition, and bartenders adopted the Crusta's sugary presentation. I'm glad they did. Cinnamon sugar makes this otherwise serious drink fun. I like fun.

COCKTAIL GLASS (5.5-7.5 OZ.)

3-4 pinches of cinnamon sugar (1:1 mixture)
for the rim of glass
1 ½ ounces spiced rum
1 ounce lemon juice, plus lemon slice
for coating rim of glass
3/4 ounce orange Curaçao
1/2 ounce simple syrup (see page 63)
Orange peel for garnish

Coat the rim of a chilled cocktail glass with cinnamon sugar by rubbing a lemon slice around the edge of the glass, then turn the glass on its side and dip into cinnamon sugar mixture, turning until it's coated all around the outside of the rim. Combine liquid ingredients in a shaker with ice and shake until cold. Strain into chilled cocktail glass. Garnish with orange peel. *Makes 1 drink.*

VODKA ESPRESSO

London bartender Dick Bradsell created this cocktail
in 1983 for a model who walked into his bar wanting
something that would "wake her up, and fuck her up."
Tall order considering that alcohol taken in sufficient
proportions has a sedative effect. (Actually, that is a
good thing, as we naturally stop drinking once we have
hit a certain point.) Still, the speedball is something
partygoers the world over admire. Today, it is Red Bull
and vodka; then it was the Vodka Espresso. I would take
the latter anytime over the former. At least it tastes
good. During the Martini craze of the 1990s, Bradsell
simplified this drink by making the ingredients equal
parts and dropping the sugar syrup, and dubbed it the
Espresso Martini.

CHILLED COCKTAIL GLASS (5.5-7.5 OZ.)

2 ounces vodka
1 ounce espresso
1/2 ounce coffee liqueur
1/4 ounce simple syrup
3 espresso beans for garnish

Combine liquid ingredients in a shaker with ice and shake until cold.
Strain into chilled cocktail glass and garnish with espresso beans.
Makes 1 drink.

TOMMY'S MARGARITA

Once you make this, you will stop with all that foolishness that abounds with orange liqueurs and sour mix. Like the classic Daiquiri, it's the simplicity of this recipe using fresh juice and agave nectar that makes it so delicious. It's the claim to fame of Tommy's, a tequila bar in San Francisco run by Julio Bermejo, that cranks this drink out by the thousands weekly for happy imbibers.

DOUBLE ROCKS GLASS (10-12 OZ.)

Salt for the rim of the glass (optional)
2 ounces tequila
1 ounce lime juice
½ ounce agave nectar
Lime wheel for garnish

Add salt to the rim of the glass if desired. Combine liquid ingredients in a shaker with ice and shake until cold. Strain over fresh ice into double rocks glass. Garnish with a lime wheel. *Makes 1 drink.*

CHOCOLATE MOJITO (ORIGINAL)

I do not know what I was thinking when I made this cocktail for the first time. Everything about it now sounds suspect to me, yet still it works. And with the addition of a chocolate straw, it was a popular order at the bar I ran at the time. I guess I've included it here as a cautionary tale for the cocktail renaissance. You can make almost anything taste good with a little experimentation, but not every creative variation is meant to become a new classic. Yes, by all means make this cocktail and enjoy it. Just don't tell them you got it from this book. My hearty thank you in advance.

COLLINS GLASS (10-12 OZ.)

6 mint leaves
½ ounce Demerara syrup
(1:1 Demerara cane sugar to water)
1 ½ ounces aged rum
½ ounce Crème de Cacao Dark
½ ounce lime juice
½ ounce papaya juice
3 ounces soda water
1 mint sprig
Dark chocolate (square or shaved as garnish)

Gently muddle leaves with Demerara syrup in mixing glass. Add spirits, juice, and a generous portion of ice into shaker and shake until cold. Strain over ice into Collins glass. Top with soda water and garnish with mint sprig. Serve with dark chocolate square or shaved chocolate as garnish. *Makes 1 drink.*

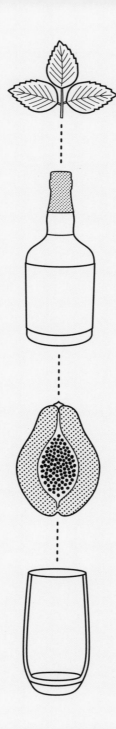

CHAPTER NINE

Oaxacan Old Fashioned
p186

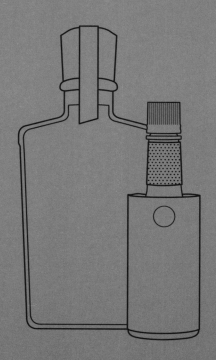

The Platinum Age is the era during which I learned to bartend. I discovered classic cocktails and the community that surrounded them, swore my fidelity to the movement, and decided to dedicate myself to becoming the best bartender in the world. In case you are wondering, I haven't gotten there yet. But shoot at the moon and land among the stars, you know. I was armed with a fail-proof Sazerac recipe, started making my own orange bitters, rediscovered D.C.'s classic cocktail, the Rickey, and could not shut up about fresh juices.

I admit that I was probably insufferable at first. And I remember the complaints of fellow bartenders: the drinks are too strong, no one could be expected to remember all these recipes, my boss won't let me use fresh juice. I was determined not to accept the excuses and neither should any other bartender. But for many, it was only a means to an end. The profession of bartending had become overrun with temps. It was not at all uncommon for bartenders to be pursuing education, music, or acting, with bartending as their side hustle. Customers deserved better. And soon they would get it.

Now before you think I just settled a score, I will be completely honest. I did not know what a jigger was. I still shook my Martinis. I thought the Rickey I made was terrible, and it was. I made a string of awful cocktails such as the Hot Cosmo (a warmed-up mix of Celestial Seasonings Cranberry Apple Zinger Herbal Tea, lemon-infused vodka, triple sec, and select spices), an Orange Julius rendition of the Bronx, and worse. Back then, the neophyte bartender was a holy terror on the world; caring, sure, but with very little instruction. We were students without teachers. A crop of now legendary bartenders were popping up throughout the country and in Washington, D.C., but many of us were still bumping around in the dark. I am sure none of us want to admit it now, but at least half the drinks we made were unpalatable.

This was a time of transition, when the new old ways would replace the now-ingrained old new ways. It was confusing because often our bar elders were the worst bartenders of the bunch. And we were stuck in the middle. I remember a bitter fight I had with an old waiter named Guy who swore up and down that the Manhattan did not have bitters in it and then, once proven wrong, argued that guests did not want bitters anyway. That kind of confusion was rampant. So those of us who counted ourselves in the movement pushed even harder. Our new enemy was vodka, flavorless drinks, shooters, sour mix, and indifference. And we started to teach each other. It would be a slow build, but we would get there and change everything.

DC DRINKS

It is always better to drink with a friend and one of my best friends and drinking buddies, Damon Fodge, was down for the cause. He was not a bartender but loved classic drinks nonetheless. One day when we were at lunch, he suggested we start a blog. I loved the idea, and so DC Drinks was born. We decided to write under pseudonyms—frankly, to say whatever the hell we wanted. I chose "Isaac Washington," after my favorite TV bartender from the Love Boat, and he picked "Lonnie Bruner," after his grandfather.

It was one of a handful of blogs at the time. We took a lot of inspiration from Portland, Oregon-based bartender Jeffrey Morgenthaler, Robert Hess, and Ted Haigh. But we wrote like a bunch of jackasses, truly. Case in point, our manifesto:

At DCDrinks we write for Drinkers, capital "D". We have scoured recipe books from 1911 for the first Jell-O shooters; We have experimented by making Creme de Menthe and still realized there is no way to make the Stinger taste remotely good; We have cried at a perfectly made Martini, cold rim beckoning our quivering lips; We have lined up 130+ proof ryes to taste and pass out in pursuit of finding the exact proof that one reaches Nirvana; We have eschewed flavorless beverages and crowned craft producers of the world king;

We have even argued how much pulp to put in a Gin & Juice; We are brothers and sisters bound to the glass, mug and cup, feverishly driven by the pursuit of drinking the very best booze we can.

Drinkers of the world: You are our people, and we are yours.

As this community grows, we rejoice that the world is right and good. However, at DCDrinks we don't care if we were read by one single solitary reader, provided that reader winces at the thought of leaving bitters out of a Manhattan, or has raced home after the pounding drudgery of the day to pour poetry in a shaker, carefully, measured by a jigger and steady hand.

But over the past year we've entertained and amused thousands of passerbys who are searching for dirty martinis, cosmos, and roofies (and, anyway, what's the f-ing difference). We appreciate your curiosity but we don't like you. We don't want you. Unless you're willing to try something better, to take a leap and reach beyond the safety of Grey Goose and soda, we despise you.

Of course, I laugh at it now. I really couldn't care less if someone drinks a vodka soda and would probably have a worse reaction toward anyone who refers to his or her drink as "poetry in a shaker," but in some ways that is how a movement works. It starts with a little fanaticism and overreaching. Then it settles into its own skin.

MUSEUM OF THE AMERICAN COCKTAIL

I can imagine a new meme being generated: there's a museum for that. Ice cream, there's a museum for that. Punk-rock band Ramones, there's a museum for that. Cocktails, there is definitely a museum for that. Founded by the DeGroffs, Dale and Jill, Robert Hess, Anistatia Miller, Jared Brown,

Chris and Laura McMillian, Ted Haigh, and Phil Greene, MOTAC as it is abbreviated, is a signpost for the history of bartending and cocktails. It is appropriately enough housed in New Orleans, in a section of the Southern Food & Beverage Museum, with a statue of nineteenth-century legend Jerry Thomas welcoming you as you enter. Curated by Ted Haigh, it has a small but poignant exhibit of the tools, style, and brands that defined the Golden Era .

I was lucky enough to be invited to the board of the museum and curated a series of seminars in Washington, D.C., with Phil Greene. We would hold seminars on everything from holiday cocktails to the hundredth anniversary of the Daiquiri, with bartenders from throughout the country participating. It was formative and helped garner enthusiasm among a public thirsty, figuratively and literally, for classic cocktails.

VESTS, BAR RULES & A PERFECTIONIST'S EYE

Milk & Honey was the first true outpost of the Platinum Age. Yes, some bars existed before it that focused on craft cocktails, but New York's Milk & Honey, opened in 2000, was altogether different. Conceived by the late, great Sasha Petraske and influenced by Japanese drinking dens, it came with a vibe and mystique that captivated the mixology world. And it was not just the drinks. Sasha's sartorial choices became as much a package of the bar world as the cadre of classic cocktails. Suddenly the magician's uniform, as we call it, of black shirts and black pants was replaced by suits, vests, fedoras, and suspenders. Not only were the drinks growing more respectable along with the garb, but so was the profession as well. Along with the new look was a new attitude. To come to the bars, you had to follow a set of prescribed rules. These were the house rules of Milk & Honey, inscribed on a bronze plaque on the bathroom door:

No name-dropping, no star fucking.
No hooting, hollering, shouting, or other loud behaviour.
No fighting, play fighting, no talking about fighting.
Gentlemen will remove their hats. Hooks are provided.
Gentlemen will not introduce themselves to ladies. Ladies,
feel free to start a conversation or ask the bartender to
introduce you. If a man you don't know speaks to you,

please lift your chin slightly and ignore him.

Do not linger outside the front door.

Do not bring anyone unless you would leave that person alone in your home. You are responsible for the behaviour of your guests.

Exit the bar briskly and silently. People are trying to sleep across the street. Please make all your travel plans and say all farewells before leaving the bar.

But all of this is not to detract from the drinks—the drinks were paramount. Ice, which for so long had been chip ice from cheap machines, once again became a central focus. (Remember that with spirits, sugar, water, and bitters, the water often comes from the ice.) It had to be large cubes for shaking and stirring and served over large ice spears or blocks. Ingredients mattered, of course, and technique was revived. Sasha not only changed the way the bar looked and felt; he also joined the best bartenders of our time in advancing the quality of drinks to a perfectionist's level.

PEGU CLUB

A few blocks away, another perfectionist opened her own New York bar in 2005, Audrey Saunders's Pegu Club, named after a 1920s British colonial social club and cocktail from colonial Burma. Though Milk & Honey may have been the outpost for the new school of mixology, Pegu Club seemed a touch more refined and mature. I still remember the first time I walked in and how the smell of citrus and booze—now familiar in cocktail bars—overtook me. The smell has replaced the more familiar odor from bars of cigarettes and beer, thankfully. It was clean and busy. The bartenders were efficient and the drinks crafted to perfection. It did not just feel like a revival bar or speakeasy. It felt like a brand-new temple—one where we worship by the glass.

Audrey was a disciple of Dale DeGroff, and among the first followers of his renaissance. She partnered with Julie Reiner, who had created another temple of mixology for the masses, Flatiron Lounge, in 2003. She also made David Embury required reading for her bartenders, which was a boon. Audrey created many amazing drinks in her own right, and is well known for her attention to detail and meticulous crafting. Pegu not only served as sacred ground but as a training ground, too. Her first class of bartenders later became among the best-known bartenders in the country: Toby Maloney, Phil Ward, Brian Miller, Jim Meehan. The rigorous initiation of bartenders and the groundswell of interest would feed New York's bar scene and branch out across the country.

THE THIRD WAVE

In some ways, this part is the trickiest to capture. When we traipse through history noting a few exceptional bartenders and places, it is inevitably an incomplete picture. There were so many people who fed the movement and created the bars that would be considered the top in the world today. Some of the names I listed deserve more than a glancing mention, but we are trying to capture the zeitgeist—the people, bars, manuals, and drinks that define an era. Rather than run down a list, I will refer to this group as the Third Wave. These were the bartenders who, from New York, San Francisco, Chicago, Boston, and D.C., among other cities, came after the first followers and shared an ever-expanding scope and ambition. Sometime in the mid-2000s, we went from dozens of revivalists to hundreds. And great new bars opened: Violet Hour in Chicago created by Toby Maloney; Eastern Standard in Boston with Jackson Cannon at the helm; PX in Alexandria, Virginia, with Todd Thrasher. And PDT in New York with a one-shift bartender from Pegu Club (who also worked at Gramercy Tavern), Jim Meehan. Though so many outposts were now opening, PDT would later become one of the most highly regarded bars in the world and its proprietor, one of the highest regarded bartenders.

THE BAR BEHIND THE PHONE BOOTH

I don't know if Jason Wilson, a spirits and wine writer, first coined this term or not, but I first heard it out of his mouth: speakcheesy. At a certain point, new bars imitating Prohibition-era speakeasies had became so saturated and gimmicky—with entrances from phone booths to sliding bookshelves—that it became an apt term. These bars seemed to re-create the conventions of Prohibition, including a dimly lit venue and suspender-snapping bartenders, but they missed one key feature of those times: during Prohibition the drinks were really bad (see the Orange Blossom if you don't believe me). The drinks they were actually serving became known as pre-Prohibition style, definitely a better descriptor.

Yet before the deluge of speakeasies, there was PDT. The name itself garnered intrigue: Please Don't Tell, with its logo bounded by an ouroboros, an ancient Egyptian symbol (later adopted by alchemists) of a snake biting its own tail. To slip through the phone booth and grab a drink there seemed in itself an achievement. But to be hosted by Jim, a gracious host indeed, felt as though you were transported. (Jim is also a natural leader in the movement and inspired this chapter title by announcing this age of drinking as the Platinum Age.) The drinks were modeled after pre-Prohibition drinks but had a modern sensibility. One of them, the Benton's Old Fashioned, was a bacon fat–washed bourbon drink created by PDT bartender Don Lee. It was a perfect summation of their repertoire—classically styled drinks that incorporated interesting ingredients or techniques. It was groundbreaking for sure, though a new style of cocktail-making would arise that surpassed it in complexity and culinary technique.

MOLECULAR MIXOLOGY

I still have no idea what to call it. Should it be called molecular mixology, culinary cocktails, modernist drinks? That is why I am just sticking with the way I first heard it: molecular mixology. You can debate whether that is a fair name or not amongst yourselves. However, it was not the name itself that impacted me or my fellow bartenders—it was the whole new world it opened. Molecular gastronomy started in innovative restaurants, though you may now hear it referred to as "modernist cuisine." The Spanish restaurant El Bulli was a pioneer, helmed by chef, magician, and veritable scientist Ferran Adrià. It incorporated chemicals and techniques derived from food science that would revolutionize fine dining: foams, gels, and spherification were all new ways to express flavor and texture. Many of the bartenders who worked in fine dining would be called to the classic cocktail movement early (including me; I worked as a sommelier at the time) and would borrow ideas from the chefs they worked with.

One such bartender was Eben Freeman. Eben worked at WD-50, a New York location for the molecular gastronomy movement, helmed by chef Wylie Dufresne. He and pastry chef Sam Mason opened Tailor restaurant in New York in 2007. There the desserts and savory dishes blurred the lines between both, and the cocktails caused a storm. Eben's Waylon, a smoked Coke and bourbon drink, presaged the smoke-in-cocktails fad by a decade and was described by writer John T. Edge as "stupefyingly, playfully great." I concur, the drink was revelatory. Cocktails were no longer bound by the past. We now had culinary cocktails that earned just as much respect for technique and craft as what was coming out of the country's most innovative kitchens. Molecular mixology became the one wholly unique cocktail trend of the Platinum Age.

TALES OF THE COCKTAIL

The question remained: how do you learn about these great ideas that were now proliferating, from speakeasies to molecular mixology? Blogs were one source, observing or sharing knowledge amongst fellow bartenders was another, but a locus of information was lacking. That void was filled by Ann Tuennerman (then Ann Rogers) who created Tales of the Cocktail, a cocktail conference in New Orleans.

Bolstered by brand money and having worked with cocktail giants Dale DeGroff, Jared Brown, Anistatia Miller, and Ted Haigh, she had the foundations of her conference. It featured a number of rising cocktail personalities—a new term for bartenders who now reached beyond the bar as educators, brand ambassadors, and general purveyors of knowledge. There were tours and seminars on just about every topic that touched the bartender's world, including history, technique, self-care, brand activations, and parties—there had to be parties.

When I first attended in 2007, it still felt cozy. Presenters could easily slip in and out of presentations, you had time to sit with friends for a drink, and it was contained mostly within the venerable New Orleans Hotel Monteleone. It's grown into a mammoth event with twenty-five thousand attendees spread throughout the French Quarter, all dedicated drinkers to brave the Big Easy in the middle of July. It's now difficult to find time to meet up with a fraction of the players. (A common joke is walking through the lobby of Monteleone, seeing someone you know and saying, "Let's meet for a drink.") I'm not complaining since it simply reflects the growth of the movement as a whole, and that it's here to stay.

B.A.R.

Are you tired of hearing about Dale DeGroff yet? You shouldn't be. His influence remains paramount in the development of craft cocktails, and a venture he started with partners David Wondrich, Doug Frost, Steve Olson, F. Paul Pacult, and Andy Seymour would become the Harvard of bartending schools—B.A.R. (Beverage Alcohol Resource). I first heard about the program when I was taking a sommelier test with Doug Frost, and I was instantly riveted. This was a chance for me to learn from the very best and to leave wine behind and return to the bar once again.

The program options have now expanded but initially there was only one, the B.A.R.-5 Day program. During five days the partners lectured on a range of topics and tested students on various spirits. Each partner added his own particular point of view: Dale's fastidiousness with drink making, David's deep dive into cocktail history, Steve's infectious love for both classic and obscure spirits, Paul's methodology for tasting spirits, and Andy's hands-on skills in bartending. Together they made up a supergroup of cocktail personalities, one that has essentially codified how we make cocktails today. The B.A.R. program helped bridge the gap between the Golden Age and the Platinum Age, and make up for some of the damage done to the profession by Prohibition.

DEATH & COMPANY

As I've mentioned before, I did not initially pass my B.A.R. test. But I would retake it along with the late Robert Cooper, who founded St-Germain, an influential spirits brand that would later be deemed "bartender's ketchup." Rob passed the test, and luckily this time, so did I. But barely. I was a sommelier at the time and bartending the B.A.R. way was brand-new to me, even if I had started to lean in that direction and learn what I could from the internet and other bartenders. Another thing was brand-new to me: New York cocktail bars. I had visited the cocktail temples, but now a new crop of bars was popping up throughout the city, especially on the Lower East Side. And then, in Death & Co., I felt as if I had found a home.

Many of New York's top bartending talent moved to (or through) Death & Co., but for me, the two bartenders who blew me away with their knowledge and attentiveness were Joaquin Simo and Alex Day. I had a million questions: Why do you shake cocktails that way? What are xocolatl mole bitters? What is V.E.P. Chartreuse? While B.A.R. provided me with the fundamentals, it was at Death & Co., where I took advanced classes. The dark interior, the intimate space, the level of skill and knowledge, and the willingness to share.

It became, in part, my model for the bar I would build in Washington, D.C., the Columbia Room. Many years later, Death & Co. owner Dave Kaplan and his now partner Alex Day would approach me about borrowing aspects from the Columbia Room for their L.A. bar Walker Inn. In all honesty, I gave them back their own ideas with a little embellishment.

Of course, there were many other bars too where I picked up knowledge. Especially at Bar Milano, where the bar program was created by Tony Abou-Ganim and included bartenders Elba Giron and Eryn Reece. I sat and took notes. Often those notes would be the titles of books you had to find at great difficulty, as the young Dale DeGroff had searched for Jerry Thomas's famous manual. Soon there would be a publishing company called Cocktail Kingdom that would reprint all of the bartending classics—akin to reassembling the historic library at Alexandria.

COCKTAIL KINGDOM

Greg Boehm and I have more in common than cocktails. Though you would never know at first glance from our hair length and cleaned-up dress, we are both huge metalheads. Still, I will wait for his book on the history of metal. In the meantime, Boehm, whose father was a publisher, decided to turn his growing library of classic cocktail books into a publishing business that would help revive classic tomes that had long been out of print. This, in itself, was incredible news to bartenders, but he also added barware to his inventory list. Barware was often super-low quality or ridiculously expensive, depending on whether it was made for commercial use or as decorative item. Cobbler shakers often stuck together. Bar spoons were incredibly cheap looking, with their red plastic tops. You probably stirred in a shaker tin rather than a traditional mixing glass. Boehm introduced beautiful, long spoons and exquisite Japanese Yarai mixing glasses. Bartenders already had the recipes, the outfit, and the attitude. Now they also had the tools.

Boehm did not stop there. He was fascinated by Japanese bartending (another thing we have in common), and held a seminar with Japanese bartending legend Kazuo Uyeda. He is one of Japan's leading barmen, owner of Tender Bar in Tokyo's Ginza district, and inventor of the now famous hard shake (a ritualized shaking technique that is supposed to impart superior texture to the drink). During the seminar held in New York, American bartenders scratched their heads at both the precision and art behind Uyeda-san's craft. He carefully opened bottles as though he was serving priceless Chateau Lafite, shook with rhythmic perfection in a rune-like pattern, and snapped the shaker after pouring as though he were a matador gently gliding by a bull and shouting, "Olé!" It marked another moment in time for the cocktail movement and our recovery from the ravages of Prohibition. Japanese bartenders, working in relative isolation for decades, represented a valuable repository of cocktail knowledge and technique. We had learned from London, we had learned from New York, and now we would learn from Tokyo and be open to the whole world.

HUMMINGBIRD TO MARS

What do you do with all this knowledge? The truth is that many bar owners did not see the worth in hand carving ice and using obscure bitters. They wanted to pump out Vodka Sodas and Dirty Martinis. They did not want the drinks to take longer; they wanted them faster and cheaper, the very antithesis of what we were now learning. So, we did what we had learned decades before from punk rock: we did it ourselves. After taking the B.A.R. program with fellow D.C. bartenders Justin Guthrie, Kevin Rogers, and Owen Thompson, we decided to open a bar within a bar in our hometown that would represent our newfound knowledge and values. We found a kindred spirit in bar owner Bill Thomas, who was (and is) obsessed with whiskey, and he allowed us to open upstairs at his bar Bourbon on Sunday and Monday, traditionally slower days. We named it Hummingbird to Mars after the now absurd 1930 statement by Texas Senator Morris Sheppard about Prohibition's staying power (see page 95) that repeal had as much chance as a hummingbird's ability "to fly to the planet Mars with the Washington Monument tied to its tail." (Repeal came just three years later.)

Mind you, we all had full-time jobs. This was extracurricular and we, or mostly Owen since he worked at Bourbon, set it up and took it down after the two shifts. We donned vests, ordered block ice, found and made our own bitters, crafted a classic cocktail menu, and issued rules for attending. Namely, you could not write about Hummingbird to Mars. What did the spirits and cocktail writer for the *Washington Post* do when receiving these rules? Just that. He wrote about it expecting to never be invited back. He wasn't, but we also shut it down. It was way too much work. Still, it was the first true cocktail bar in Washington, D.C. proper since the revival, and showed us the possibilities. It also helped to garner a community. The few D.C. bartenders bumping around in the dark solidified into its own local movement.

DC CRAFT BARTENDERS GUILD

At this point, I started researching the history of D.C. bartending and, especially, the Rickey—D.C.'s signature contribution to the cocktail world. Along with author Garrett Peck and my business partner Angie Fetherston (then Angie Salame), we succeeded in getting it declared as Washington, D.C.'s official cocktail. During my reading, I came across an article in the *Washington Post* from September 16, 1928, entitled, "The Lost Legion." It was eloquently and lengthily subtitled: "A Lachrymose Requiem for the Stalwarts in the Service of the Siphon Who Have Drifted Into More Prosaic Pursuits Since the Aridity Imposed by Volsteadism—a Former Maitre of the Mahogany Recalls Glories of the Day That is Gone and Its Cocktails, Rickies and Fizzes With It—What Has Become of the Famous Bartenders Who Hobnobbed With World Leaders in Politics, Business and the Arts in the Palmy Days?"

I was blown away by learning the stories of so many great bartenders from our city's history, and the "Aridity Imposed by Volsteadism" that had led to the loss of their jobs. I was ever more determined to bolster our community. So I reached out to Gina Chersevani, one of D.C.'s top bartenders, and we discussed plans to create a guild. It would be entirely for us. We had no intention of joining the national and international guilds.

Those guilds have since become an important part of the larger bartending community, but in 2008, D.C. felt somewhat isolated, and in fact, it was. At least from the U.S. Bartenders Guild and International Bartenders Association. Ten original members got together after Gina and I had that initial call and we laid down the ideas that would form the D.C. Craft Bartenders Guild. Those members were: Gina Chersevani, Owen Thomson, Kevin Rogers, Justin Guthrie, Chantal Tseng, Kat Bangs, Dan Searing, Adam Bernbach, my brother Tom Brown, and I. We drafted the following guidelines for the guild:

PROFESSIONALISM

To establish the highest level of professionalism, cooperation and exemplary service amongst its members and the industry as a whole.

KNOWLEDGE
To encourage the dissemination of knowledge and innovation in craft bartending with a focus on hospitality.

HOSPITALITY
To promote the District of Columbia as a preeminent city for craft bartending with a focus on hospitality.

OUTREACH
To contribute to the growing national and international community of craft bartenders.

CIVIC ENGAGEMENT
To engage the District's alcohol and bar regulatory environment in a way that benefits the D.C. Craft Bartenders Guild and its members and to work with the community to establish the norms of alcohol safety.

Quite the difference from my rabble-rousing blogging days. But the soldiers that formed the first, second, and third wave of the cocktail movement were now a professional community. I mark this as the point where there was no going back. This was no longer a trend or a cutesy movement within the culinary world. Owners could not ignore their staff and customers anymore. Cocktails were ascendant and no longer relegated to a few keys cities. From here, they would spread to city after city through the force of their own momentum.

THE INDIANA JONES OF COCKTAIL INGREDIENTS

Now, the trick was to dig deeper. Sure, you could read about how to make an Aviation, a drink that made its debut in 1916, four years before Prohibition. But you were missing a key ingredient—crème de violette—to make it with (and without it, the Aviation doesn't have the sky-blue tint that likely provided its name). You cheated with substandard ingredients as you tried to make it yourself, but it was to no avail. Someone was going to have to resurrect these obscure cocktail ingredients, and that someone was a bespectacled "Indiana Jones of Cocktail Ingredients," also known as Eric Seed. He began his quest in New York, though his home is in Minneapolis, by talking to bartenders about what they were looking for and then hunted down the source. Products that had been long lost started to appear behind bars: crème de violette, Batavia arrack, Swedish punsch. We could now make an Aviation, Jupiter, and Arrack punch.

I met Eric after hounding him to bring crème de violette to D.C., and we instantly struck up a friendship. He asked me what bartenders were looking for and I said, Dolin Vermouth, a vermouth from Chambéry, France, that was dry and delicate, making exceptional Dry Martinis. Shortly after, I phoned him about some products and he said, "Guess where I am: Chambéry." He imported Dolin, and now bartenders had a new vermouth staple behind the bar. They started acting accordingly too, properly storing it in the fridge once opened as the fortified wine that it is.

SMOKE & RYE

The search for new ingredients became half the fun of bartending. Learning about where the product came from, who made it, and sharing that knowledge with guests indoctrinated a whole new group of guests into the cocktail world. We had reached out beyond cocktail nerds and now became fair game for foodies and the broader cocktail set. The culture grew, and with it, consumer influence. The spirits that perhaps best exemplify this growth are mezcal and rye.

Mezcal is an agave spirit from Mexico that is the overarching category for tequila. Tequila is a shortened name for what used to be called "mezcal de tequila." However, mezcal is more often made in a traditional manner that gives more character to the agaves. (Tequila only uses one variety of agave where mezcal uses many more.) The person who spearheaded mezcal in the United States, Ron Cooper, did so long before the cocktail movement had reached its peak. He started a company selling artisanal mezcals from Oaxaca called Del Maguey. But it was with the aid of company co-owner Steve Olson and fellow evangelists that mezcal became a handshake among bartenders, like a shot of the Italian amaro Fernet Branca. Served in a clay cup with the refrain "Stigibeu," (a toast of the indigenous Zapotec civilization of Oaxaca that roughly translates "to the collective lifeforce"), you expected to drink mezcal at the end of the night (or mid-shift). It was what bartenders did. The smoky, earthy finish became so familiar that mezcal-themed cocktail bars opened as well. King among them was Mayahuel in New York, helmed by former Pegu Club and Death & Co, bartender, Phil Ward.

The other spirit that captivated bartenders was rye whiskey. When I tried to make my first Sazerac, there was not a rye on the shelf. Sure they existed, but they were not called for. Rye whiskey had been an essential ingredient in early American cocktails, and was widely available up until Prohibition. Over the past decade, bartenders and cocktail evangelists helped revive the demand for it, and it's since grown in sales over 500 percent. You can expect any bar worth a shaker of salt to have at least half a dozen rye whiskeys, including small-batch ryes that go for hundreds of dollars. At my brother Tom Brown's D.C. bar, the Passenger, he sold over six thousand bottles of Old Overholt in five short years. (Well, maybe they were not all sold.) Still, the growth was driven by bartenders and consumer demand. We can point with pride, as bartenders and cocktail nerds, and say, "We did that."

SHERRY

The one spiritous liquor, actually fortified wine, that came back to the bar but has yet to gain the appeal of rye and mezcal among drinkers is sherry. I know, because I opened a sherry bar called Mockingbird Hill in D.C. in 2013. It was a passion product filled with things I loved, including a dizzying array of sherries. At one point we had over one hundred sherries, most available by the glass. For a small set of sherry lovers, it was a boon. For those who understood cocktails but had yet to make the leap to sherry, they scratched their heads. Many stopped in and tried sherry but as a regular haunt, they passed on it. I was heartbroken. I had spent time with families in Jerez who produced sherry, hand sold glass after glass, and spoke to anyone I could about this beautiful, traditional product that had thousands of years of history and was carried over on Christopher Columbus's journey.

Mockingbird Hill closed a few years after to house a series of pop-up bars. Yet, two hundred fifty years after having been a staple of the American colonies, it is at least gaining ground as an ingredient for cocktails—there is even a yearly Vinos de Jerez contest for the best sherry cocktail led by Steve Olson.

Sherry is a handshake among bartenders, and some of the same people who once scratched their heads at what we were doing at Mockingbird Hill now stop me at events to reminisce about the great sherries they tried and, gasp, introduced to friends. As a whisper campaign, sherry has made inroads, and I am sure there will be more sherry cocktails and even sherry bars outside of Spain that will arrive and succeed. And, as a side note, though we ended our own sherry bar experiment at Mockingbird Hill, we still have sherry cocktails at its replacement, P.U.B., the Pop-Up Bar, which houses rotating holiday and pop-culture themes. In fact, we sell more sherry than ever that way.

Maybe the only remedy to cure the sweet, Granny-like reputation to which many people have condemned sherry is by bringing it to guests through the back door, via a well-balanced, interesting, and delicious cocktail. I guess that is not so much different from early Americans and the manner in which they drank. They liked their sherry mixed, too. In fact, we have always loved a good cocktail, no matter how much it changes over time, no matter how much it ebbs and flows, falls and rises to prominence. The cocktail is delicious. It is something we should love too—after all, we invented it.

OAXACAN
OLD FASHIONED

The Oaxacan Old Fashioned has quickly become a new classic, created by bartender Phil Ward while he was at Death & Co. in New York City. Ward would later open the bar Mayahuel in the East Village, once a temple to agave-spirit cocktails. He also made the trip to western Jalisco with me and was always ready with a Victoria pilsner and mezcal in hand. His Oaxacan Old Fashioned is singularly perfect, drawing from the form of the classic, original cocktail but weighing the sometimes smoky and more aggressive taste of mezcal against the more refined, aged taste of reposado tequila. This is definitely a sipper, and one that can introduce the neophyte to mezcal cocktails.

DOUBLE ROCKS GLASS (10-12 OZ.)

1 ½ ounces reposado tequila
½ ounce mezcal
1 barspoon (or 1 teaspoon) agave nectar
2 dashes aromatic bitters
Orange peel for garnish

Combine liquid ingredients in mixing glass with ice and stir until chilled. Strain into double rocks glass with single, large ice cube. Express oils from orange peel by holding the exocarp, or outside of peel, downward by both ends and twist over the drink, and then add peel to drink. *Makes 1 drink.*

PENICILLIN

The Penicillin was created by bartender Sam Ross at
Milk & Honey in New York. It's often referred to as a
cure-all for a very good reason. Despite the call for
Scotch, it's pretty universally considered delicious
among non-whiskey drinkers. There's something about
that honey-ginger syrup that tempers the bite of
whisky. Just like the Oaxacan Old Fashioned, this is sort
of a gateway drug. Still insist you don't like Scotch? One
sip will change all that.

DOUBLE ROCKS GLASS (10-12 OZ.)

2 ounces blended scotch whiskey
¾ ounce lemon juice
¾ ounce honey-ginger syrup (recipe follows)
1 barspoon (or 1 teaspoon) Islay single malt Scotch
Candied ginger for garnish

Combine liquid ingredients in a shaker with ice and shake until cold.
Strain over fresh ice in double rocks glass. Garnish with candied ginger.
Makes 1 drink.

HONEY-GINGER SYRUP

Combine 1 cup honey and 2.7 ounces hot water. Then combine this
mixture with 1 cup ginger syrup (2 parts raw ginger juice to 1.5 part
caster sugar). Transfer syrup to a sealed container and refrigerate
overnight. The syrup will keep for approximately one month in a sealed
container in the refrigerator.

GIN GIN MULE

Cocktails that are fun to say get bonus points in my book. Don't get me wrong; this is a serious drink— I'm not trying to undermine that—but the name, plus ginger and mint also say party drink to me. Created by Audrey Saunders at Pegu Club in New York City, this drink benefits from ginger, a beloved ingredient in cocktails for its pleasing bite. (Do yourself a favor and make the ginger beer yourself—Audrey's recipe is given here—but if you absolutely have to use the canned stuff, reduce the simple syrup to ½ ounce.)

HIGHBALL (10. OZ.)

¾ ounce fresh lime juice
1 ounce simple syrup (see page 63)
2 mint sprigs (1 for muddling, 1 reserved for garnish)
1 ounce homemade ginger beer (see recipe below)
1 ¾ oz gin (one with a strong juniper profile is best)
Lime wheel and candied ginger for garnish.

Combine lime juice, simple syrup, and 1 mint sprig into a mixing glass. Muddle well. Add gin, ginger beer, and ice. Shake well, strain into a highball glass, and serve with a long straw. *Makes 1 drink.*

HOMEMADE GINGER BEER (YIELD 1 CUP)

Boil 1 cup water. Remove from heat and add 2 tablespoons grated ginger and ½ teaspoon lime juice. Cover and let stand for 1 hour. Add 1 teaspoon light brown sugar, stir, and strain through a fine mesh sieve, pushing on ginger solids to express ginger extract. Bottle and refrigerate.

DARKSIDE

D.C. bartender Adam Bernbach used to run a unique cocktail program out of Bar Pilar called Cocktail Sessions. Guests could cozy up to the bar and order a cocktail tasting where Adam would fix three original cocktails using twists on classics. One of my favorite drinks to make it out of those sessions is the Darkside. Chinato was historically considered an aromatized wine like vermouth and consumed that way. It combines herbs, spices, and quinine bark, the same ingredient found in tonic that gives it a bitter edge. Chinato is now often relegated to pairing with chocolate (and it does pair amazingly well with dark chocolate), but here its original function is restored. It's a brilliant drink.

COCKTAIL GLASS (5.5-7.5 OZ.)

2 ½ ounces dry gin
¾ ounce Barolo Chinato
3 dashes Peychaud's Bitters
Cherry for garnish

Combine all ingredients except garnish in a mixing glass or shaker with ice and stir until cold. Strain into chilled cocktail glass and garnish with a cherry. *Makes 1 drink.*

SALAD DAYS SOUR
(ORIGINAL)

I went for the easy pun here: celery, carrots, eggs.
But the song *Salad Days* by Minor Threat was actually
playing in my head. Celery is delicious in pisco; it adds
a subtle vegetal note to the clear brandy. I've never
been crazy about cinnamon—it makes me want to
cough—but not when burnt. Its smell is so welcoming,
like the spice bags people use during the holidays to
give their homes a festive smell. I've probably made
more of this drink than almost any other drink in my
life. Be warned: People always come back for another.

COCKTAIL GLASS (5.5-7.5 OZ.)

1 ½ oz. celery-infused pisco*
¾ oz. lemon juice
¾ oz. simple syrup
1 egg white
Cinnamon ash** and carrot confetti*** for garnish

Combine pisco, lemon, simple syrup, and egg white in a shaker with
ice and shake until cold. Strain into chilled glass and garnish with
cinnamon ash (try to use the ash to draw a line down the middle of the
drink) and carrot confetti. *Makes 1 drink.*

*Chop 2–3 stalks of celery and add to pisco. Allow to sit for 45 minutes,
then strain out celery.
**Burn loose cinnamon with a pastry torch in a large metal bowl.
*** Slice small peels off of a carrot (we use different colored ones),
then soak them in ice water until they curl.

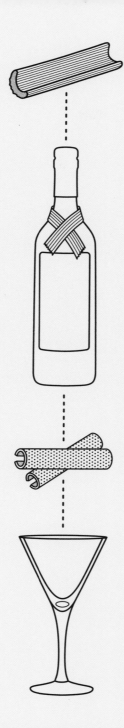

A SPIRITED TIMELINE
OF AMERICAN HISTORY

N.B. GENERAL HISTORY SET IN CAPITALS.
Cocktail history set in italics.

– *ca. 7000 bce – first recorded
discovery of chemically authenticated
alcohol in jiahu, china.*
– *2000 bce – aztecs drink pulque made
from agave plants.*
– *350 bce – aristotle writes about
the desalination of sea water, an
early distillation technique.*
– *800 ce – persian alchemist jabir
ibn hayyan (geber) develops
alembic still for distillation.*
– *1492 – Columbus arrives in the
Americas bearing sherry.*
– *1585 – Roanoke settlers brew an
ale out of corn.*
– 1607 – JAMESTOWN ESTABLISHED AS
THE FIRST PERMANENT ENGLISH
COLONY IN NORTH AMERICA.
– 1619 – ENSLAVED AFRICANS FIRST
ARRIVE IN VIRGINIA COLONY.
– 1620 – PILGRIMS' MAYFLOWER LANDS
AT PLYMOUTH ROCK.
– *1620 – English colonist George Thorpe
writes of distilling spirits from corn in
Henricus, Virginia.*
– 1630 – PURITANS ARRIVING ON
ARBELLA FOUND MASSACHUSETTS
BAY COLONY.
– 1673 – BOSTON PASTOR INCREASE
MATHER PUBLISHES SERMONS,
WO TO DRUNKARDS.
– 1733 – MOLASSES ACT IMPOSED BY

THE BRITISH PARLIAMENT, WHICH
TAXED MOLASSES FROM NON-BRITISH
COLONIES.
– *1737 – Benjamin Franklin publishes
"The Drinkers Dictionary" in the
Pennsylvania Gazette, compiling
over 200 synonyms for drunkenness.*
– *1755 – George Washington loses
his first political election for not
treating voters to enough booze.*
– 1773 – BOSTON TEA PARTY.
– 1776 – DECLARATION OF INDEPENDENCE
IS SIGNED AND AMERICA DECLARES ITS
INDEPENDENCE FROM GREAT BRITAIN
– 1781 – BRITISH SURRENDER AT
YORKTOWN, EFFECTIVELY ENDING
AMERICAN REVOLUTION.
– 1783 – TREATY OF PARIS SIGNED,
OPENING UP LANDS WEST OF
APPALACHIAN MOUNTAINS TO
SCOTCH-IRISH SETTLERS AND THEIR
WHISKEY.
– *1784 – Benjamin Rush publishes
An Inquiry into the Effects of
Spirituous Liquors.*
– 1788 – GEORGE WASHINGTON, A LOVER
OF MADEIRA WINE, ELECTED FIRST U.S.
PRESIDENT.
– *1794 – George Washington leads militia to
quell the Whiskey Rebellion, which
protested the imposition of a tax on
distilled spirits.*
– *1797 – Washington establishes a distillery
at Mount Vernon.*
– 1800 – THOMAS JEFFERSON, A
CONNOISSEUR OF EUROPEAN WINES
AND ADVOCATE OF AMERICAN
WINE, IS ELECTED PRESIDENT.

– *1803 – The term "cocktail" first appears in print in America in New Hampshire's Farmer's Cabinet.*

– *1806 – Cocktail first defined in print in The Balance, and Columbian Repository.*

– *1806 – Frederic Tudor, the "Ice King," makes his first ice shipment from Massachusetts to Martinique.*

– 1814 – THE BRITISH INVADE AMERICA DURING THE WAR OF 1812, BURNING THE WHITE HOUSE AND CAPITOL BUILDING IN WASHINGTON, D.C.

– 1825 – ERIE CANAL OPENS.

– *1826 – Minister Lyman Beecher co-founds the American Temperance Society (ATS) in Boston.*

– *1826 – First mention in print of Orsamus Willard—aka, "the Napoleon of Bar-Keepers" working at City Hotel in New York City.*

– 1826 – EDGAR ALLAN POE ATTENDS THE UNIVERSITY OF VIRGINIA.

– *1829 – Inauguration of Andrew Jackson turns rowdy at White House because of whiskey punch.*

– *1830 – Aeneas Coffey invents the column still in Scotland, which increases efficiency of distillation.*

– 1832 – FANNY TROLLOPE PUBLISHES THE DOMESTIC MANNERS OF THE AMERICANS.

– *1833 – Frederic Tudor successfully delivers ice to Calcutta, India.*

– 1842 – CHARLES DICKENS TRAVELS THROUGHOUT U.S. AND PUBLISHES AMERICAN NOTES.

– 1849 – GOLD IS DISCOVERED IN CALIFORNIA.

– 1849 – EDGAR ALLAN POE DIES.

– 1854 – HENRY DAVID THOREAU PUBLISHES WALDEN.

– *1856 – Term "mixologist" first appears in print in New York's Knickerbocker Magazine.*

– *1860 – Jerry P. Thomas opens his first bar in New York City.*

– 1861 – ABRAHAM LINCOLN ELECTED PRESIDENT. AMERICAN CIVIL WAR BEGINS WITH THE FIRING ON FORT SUMTER, SOUTH CAROLINA.

– *1862 – Jerry Thomas publishes the first cocktail book, The Bar-Tender's Guide: How to Mix Drinks: Or, The Bon Vivant's Companion.*

– 1863 – ABRAHAM LINCOLN ISSUES THE EMANCIPATION PROCLAMATION.

– 1865 – THE CIVIL WAR ENDS; SLAVERY IS ABOLISHED WITH THE 13TH AMENDMENT.

– 1866 – MARK TWAIN PUBLISHES THE ADVENTURES OF TOM SAWYER.

– 1874 – WOMEN'S CHRISTIAN TEMP-ERANCE UNION (WCTU) FOUNDED.

– *1882 – Harry Johnson publishes The New and Improved Bartender's Manual: Or How to Mix Drinks of the Present Style.*

– *1882 – The Manhattan cocktail appears in print.*

– *1885 – Jerry Thomas dies in New York City; his obituary appears in New York Times, New York Post, New York World, among others.*

– *1888 – Martini cocktail recipe first appears in print.*

– *1892 – William "The Only William" Schmidt publishes The Flowing Bowl: When and What to Drink.*

– 1896 – First Daiquiri served by American engineer Jennings Cox in Cuba.

– 1898 – SPANISH-AMERICAN WAR BEGINS AFTER SINKING OF U.S.S. MAINE IN HAVANA HARBOR.

– 1900 – Carry A. Nation smashes her first bar in Kansas. The next year she picks up her trademark hatchet to destroy bars as part of her temperance crusade.

– 1909 – The Daiquiri arrives at the Army and Navy Club in Washington, D.C.

– 1912 – TITANIC SINKS ON ITS MAIDEN VOYAGE.

– 1917 – U.S. ENTERS WORLD WAR I.

– 1917 – Prohibition begins early in Washington, D.C. with the Bone Dry Act.

– 1917 – Tom Bullock becomes the first African-American to publish a cocktail book with The Ideal Bartender.

– 1919 – THE GREAT MOLASSES FLOOD OCCURS IN BOSTON.

– 1919 – The 18th Amendment, establishing Prohibition, is ratified.

– 1920 – Prohibition takes effect nationwide on January 16.

– 1920 – WOMEN GAIN THE RIGHT TO VOTE WITH THE RATIFICATION OF THE 19TH AMENDMENT.

– 1922 – Harry MacElhone of Harry's Bar in Paris publishes Harry's ABC of Mixing Cocktails.

– 1925 – F. SCOTT FITZGERALD PUBLISHES THE GREAT GATSBY.

– 1926 – ERNEST HEMINGWAY PUBLISHES THE SUN ALSO RISES.

– 1927 – Harry MacElhone publishes Barflies and Cocktails.

– 1927 – CHARLES LINDBERGH ARRIVES IN PARIS AFTER THE FIRST SOLO FLIGHT ACROSS ATLANTIC.

– 1929 – THE STOCK MARKET CRASHES ON OCTOBER 29, STARTING THE GREAT DEPRESSION.

– 1930 – Harry Craddock publishes the Savoy Cocktail Book.

– 1932 – FDR, A LOVER OF MARTINIS, IS ELECTED PRESIDENT.

– 1933 – Prohibition repealed with the 21st Amendment.

– 1933 – Ernest Raymond Beaumont Gantt—aka "Don the Beachcomber" opens "Don's Beachcomber" in Hollywood.

– 1934 – Victor Jules Bergeron, Jr. opens Hinky Dink's in Oakland, which will become Trader Vic's.

– 1934 – Zombie cocktail created by Don the Beachcomber.

– 1941 – WORLD WAR II BEGINS FOR AMERICA AFTER THE BOMBING OF PEARL HARBOR.

– 1944 – Trader Vic's introduces its Mai Tai.

– 1945 – END OF WORLD WAR II AND FOUNDING OF THE UNITED NATIONS.

– 1946 – Victor Bergeron publishes the first Tiki cocktail book, Trader Vic's Book of Food and Drink.

– 1948 – David A. Embury publishes The Fine Art of Mixing Drinks.

– 1948 – Giuseppe Cipriani serves the first Bellini at Harry's Bar in Venice.

– 1959 – HAWAII BECOMES AMERICA'S FIFTIETH STATE.

– *1960 – John F. Kennedy, a lover of Daiquiris, elected president.*

– 1962 – CUBAN MISSILE CRISIS.

– 1963 – PRESIDENT KENNEDY IS ASSASSINATED.

– *1965 – Alan Stillman opens the first T.G.I. Fridays in NYC as a singles bar.*

– *1967 – Vodka surpasses gin in sales in America.*

– 1968 – MARTIN LUTHER KING, JR. AND ROBERT F. KENNEDY ARE ASSASSINATED.

– 1969 – NEIL ARMSTRONG AND BUZZ ALDRIN WALK ON THE MOON.

– 1974 – RICHARD NIXON, A FAN OF TIKI DRINKS, RESIGNS FROM THE PRESIDENCY.

– 1976 – AMERICA CELEBRATES ITS BICENTENNIAL.

– *1976 – Vodka overtakes whiskey as America's favorite alcohol.*

– *1984 – Heywood Gould publishes Cocktail.*

– *1984 – Peachtree Schnapps introduced by DeKuyper, and popularizes the Fuzzy Navel.*

– 1987 – STOCK MARKET CRASHES.

– *1987 – Dale DeGroff—aka, King Cocktail—begins working at The Rainbow Room.*

– *1987 – Sex on the Beach likely born in Fort Lauderdale during spring break season.*

– *1988 – Cocktail the movie is released, starring Tom Cruise.*

– 1991 – END OF THE COLD WAR.

– 1991 – WORLD WIDE WEB IS BORN.

– 1992 – BILL CLINTON, A FAN OF THE SNAKEBITE (PART LAGER, PART CIDER) DURING HIS COLLEGE DAYS, IS ELECTED PRESIDENT.

– *1993 – William Grimes publishes Straight Up or On the Rocks.*

– *1995 – Madonna photographed drinking a Cosmopolitan at the Rainbow Room.*

– *1999 – Sasha Petraske opens Milk & Honey in New York.*

– 2001 – AMERICA ATTACKED ON 9/11.

– *2003 – Julie Reiner opens Flatiron Lounge in New York.*

– *2003 – Ann Rogers (later, Ann Tuennerman) starts Tales of the Cocktail in New Orleans.*

– 2005 – HURRICANE KATRINA DEVASTATES NEW ORLEANS.

– *2005 – Audrey Saunders opens Pegu Club in New York.*

– *2007 – David Wondrich publishes Imbibe!*

– *2007 – Ravi DeRossi and David Kaplan open Death & Co in New York.*

– *2007 – Jim Meehan opens PDT (Please Don't Tell) in New York.*

– 2008 – BARACK OBAMA, A FAN OF BEER, ELECTED AS FIRST AFRICAN-AMERICAN PRESIDENT.

– *2008 – Museum of the American Cocktail opens in New Orleans, started by Dale and Jill DeGroff and other cocktail luminaries.*

– *2008 – D.C. Craft Bartenders Guild founded.*

– *2009 – Derek Brown opens the Columbia Room in the Passenger Bar in Washington, D.C.*

– *2015 – The U.S. National Archives creates the exhibit "Spirited Republic: Alcohol in American History." Derek Brown is named Chief Spirits Advisor, and leads a 10-part master class on the cocktail.*

– *2016 – Derek Brown opens up the second iteration of the Columbia Room in Washington, D.C.*

– **Angostura Bitters**: Aromatic bitters created in 1824 in the town of Angostura, Venezuela, by German Dr. Johann Siegert for stomach ailments, now produced in Trinidad. They are considered the bitters standard.

– **Boston shaker**: A two-piece shaker made of one large cup and one small cup that, when fitted together, form a seal.

– **Bourbon**: American whiskey made of at least 51 percent corn and aged in new, charred oak barrels. Bourbon was recognized as a "distinctive product of the United States" by Congress in 1964.

– **Cobbler (drink)**: Drink made with spirits or fortified wine, sweetened, poured over ice, and topped with seasonal fruit. The Sherry Cobbler helped popularize the straw.

– **Cobbler (shaker)**: A three-piece shaker that has a large cup, lid, cover, and built-in strainer.

– **Cointreau**: A French, orange-flavored liqueur known as the original triple-sec.

– **Collins**: A highball-style drink that most frequently mixes gin and lemon juice (Tom Collins) with soda water and sugar, but sometimes uses Bourbon or other spirits.

– **Curaçao**: An orange-flavored liqueur originally made on the island of Curaçao from sour oranges.

– **Dry shake**: Shaking a cocktail first without ice for greater aeration, often used for drinks with egg whites or cream.

– **Falernum**: A liqueur or syrup sweetener flavored with ginger, lime, almonds, and other spices, popular in tiki drinks. It is known commercially as the liqueur John D. Taylor's Velvet Falernum.

– **Fizz**: A Collins served without ice and topped with soda.

– **Flip**: Originally a colonial drink of beer, rum, and sugar heated with a loggerhead; later a drink that combines a spirit or fortified wine, sugar, and egg, and is served with grated nutmeg.

– **Hard shake**: A stylized shaking technique invented by Japanese bartender Kazuo Uyeda, intended to better aerate and mix the cocktail.

– **Hawthorne strainer**: A circular ice strainer with a spring around the edge of the rim, often used for shaken drinks.

– **Highball**: One of the simplest of mixed drinks, made from a base spirit, ice, and soda of some type, e.g. Jack & Coke, Gin & Tonic, etc.

– **Jigger**: A handheld measuring device, typically indicating anywhere between ¼ ounce to 2 ounces; also a unit of measurement, indicating 1½ ounces.

– **Julep strainer**: A perforated metal spoon strainer often used for stirred drinks.

– **Madeira**: A fortified wine produced in the Portuguese Madeira archipelago, popular in America during the colonial period.

– **Orgeat**: A sweet syrup often used in tiki drinks, typically made of almonds, rose, or orange water.

– **Peychaud's Bitters**: A popular bitters created by Antoine Peychaud in 1830s New Orleans, with a distinct anise flavor. It is an integral ingredient of the Sazerac.

– **Pisco**: A unaged brandy originating from Peru or Chile, popularized in Pisco Sours and Pisco Punch.

– **Port**: A sweet fortified dessert wine from Portugal.

– **Roll**: A method of mixing by pouring a drink back and forth between two shaker tins.

– **Simple syrup**: A sugar solution made by combining equal parts sugar and water. Rich simple syrup is made by combining 2 parts sugar to 1 part water.

– **Sling**: A mixture of spirit, sugar, and water. The early cocktail was known as a "bittered sling."

– **Smash**: A combination of spirit, seasonal fruit, herbs, and ice.

– **Sour**: A drink typically made of a spirit, sweetener, and citrus, such as the Daiquiri or the Whiskey Sour.

– **Sour mix**: A mix of souring ingredients, made of fresh or artificial flavors, that replaced individual citrus during the Dark Ages of the cocktail.

– **Swizzle**: A refreshing cocktail filled with crushed ice and cooled by stirring with a swizzle stick, a branch from *Quararibea turbinata*, known as the swizzle stick tree.

– **Tiki**: A style of cocktails with Polynesian flair but Caribbean origins that emerged in California in the late 1930s.

– **Vermouth**: An aromatized, fortified wine originating from Turin, Italy, in the eighteenth century. The most typical categories are referred to as sweet and dry, alternatively called Italian or French and red or white, though those designations are confusing as vermouth is produced in both countries and both colors are somewhat sweet.

– **Whisk(e)y**: A grain-based distillate that is typically aged. Irish and American whiskies are spelled with an e, with a few exceptions, while Scottish whisky is without an e.

SOURCES

– Abou-Ganim, Tony. *The Modern Mixologist: Contemporary Classic Cocktails*. Evanston, IL: Surrey Books, 2010. Mary Elizabeth Faulkner, contributor.

– Anburey, Thomas. *Travels Through the Interior Parts of America, in Two Volumes*. Volume 2. Boston and New York: Houghton Mifflin Company, 1923.

– Bass, Penelope. "History Lesson: The Bloody Mary." *Imbibe*, February 23, 2017.

– Berry, Jeff. *Beachbum Berry Remixed: A Gallery of Tiki Drinks*. San Jose, CA: SLG Publishing, 2009.

– *Beachbum Berry's Potions of the Caribbean*. New York: Cocktail Kingdom, 2013.

– *Beachbum Berry's Sippin' Safari: In Search of the Great "Lost" Tropical Drink Recipes . . . and the People Behind Them*. San Jose, CA: SLG Publishing, 2007.

– Bullen, Claire. "Dick Bradsell and the Origins of London's Cocktail Revival." *Gin Culture*, March 2017.

– Bustar, Bruce I. *Spirited Republic: Alcohol in American History*. College Park, MD: National Archives and Records Administration, 2015.

– Byron, O. H. *The Modern Bartenders' Guide*, Frenchtown, NJ: Excelsior, 1884.

– Cate, Martin, and Rebecca Cate. *Smuggler's Cove: Exotic Cocktails, Rum, and the Cult of Tiki*. Emeryville, CA: Ten Speed Press, 2016.

– Cheevers, Susan. *Drinking in America: Our Secret History*. New York: Twelve, 2016.

– Clarke, Paul. *The Cocktail Chronicles: Navigating the Cocktail Renaissance with Jigger, Shaker & Glass*. Nashville, TN: Spring House Press, 2015.

– "The Kangaroo, a.k.a. Vodka Martini Recipe." *Serious Eats*, May 2010.

– "Vodka Makes a Comeback." *Imbibe*, February 10, 2010.

– Craddock, Harry. *The Savoy Cocktail Book*. London: Pavilion Books, 2011.

– Curtis, Wayne. "The Bigot Who Wrote a Cocktail Bible." *Daily Beast*, August 3, 2017.

– *And a Bottle of Rum: A History of the New World in Ten Cocktails*. New York: Broadway Books, 2007.

– DeFerrari, John. *Historic Restaurants of Washington, D.C.: Capital Eats*. Stroud, U.K.: The History Press, 2013.

– Difford, Simon. "Daiquiri Cocktail - History & story of its creation." *Difford's Guide for Discerning Drinkers*.

– "Dick Bradsell." *Difford's Guide for Discerning Drinkers*.

– "Martini Cocktail and its evolution." *Difford's Guide for Discerning Drinkers*.

– Embury, David A. *The Fine Art of Mixing Drinks: The Classic Guide to the Cocktail*. New York: Mud Puddle Inc., 2008. (Foreword by Robert Hess, with a contribution from Audrey Saunders.)

– Escalante, Adelfo, et al. "Pulque,

a Traditional Mexican Alcoholic Fermented Beverage: Historical, Microbiological, and Technical Aspects." *Frontiers in Microbiology*, June 30, 2016.

– Felten, Eric. "A Cock(tail) 'n' Bull Story." *Wall Street Journal*, June 9, 2007.

– Fitzgerald De Roos, Frederick. *Personal Narrative of Travels in the United States and Canada in 1826: With Remarks on the Present State of the American Navy*. London: William H. Ainsworth, 1827.

– Gochman, Samuel R, et al. "Alcohol discrimination and preferences in two species of nectar-feeding primate." *Royal Society Open Science 3*, no. 7 (July 2016).

– Graysmith, Robert. "The Adventures of the Real Tom Sawyer." *Smithsonian*, October 2012.

– Greene, Philip. *The Manhattan: The Story of the First Modern Cocktail with Recipes*. New York: Sterling Epicure, 2016.

– "Toasting Hemingway's Paris With a Jack Rose." *Daily Beast*, September 13, 2018.

– *To Have and Have Another: A Hemingway Cocktail Companion.* New York: TarcherPerigee, 2015.

– Grimes, William. *Straight Up or On the Rocks: The Story of the American Cocktail*. New York: North Point Press, 2002.

– Guarino, Ben. "Earliest evidence of wine found in giant, 8,000-year-old

jars." *Washington Post*, November 13, 2017.

– Hahn, Fritz. "Rock-a-Hula Baby While You Still Can." *Washington Post*, February 13, 2004.

– Haigh, Ted aka Dr. Cocktail. *Vintage Spirits and Forgotten Cocktails, From the Alamagoozlum to the Zombie and Beyond*. Beverly, MA: Quarry Books, 2009.

– Hand Meacham, Sarah. *Every Home a Distillery: Alcohol, Gender, and Technology in the Colonial Chesapeake*. Baltimore, MD: John Hopkins University Press, 2009.

– Hariot, Thomas. *A briefe and true report of the new found land of Virginia*, 1588.

– Hayden, Brian, Neil Canuel, and Jennifer Shanse. "What Was Brewing in the Natufian? An Archaeological Assessment of Brewing Technology in the Epipaleolithic." *Journal of Archaeological Method and Theory 20*, no. 1 (March 2013).

– Huckelbridge, Dane. *Bourbon: A History of the American Spirit*. New York: William Morrow Paperbacks, 2015.

– Janzen, Emma. "Audrey Saunders on the Evolution of the Cocktail Movement." *Imbibe*, May 2016.

– Johnson, Harry. *New and Improved Illustrated Bartender's Manual: Or How to Mix Drinks of the Present Style*, 1888.

– Kent, Charles W. "Poe's Student Days at the University of Virginia." *Bookman*

13, no. 5 (July 1901).

– Lender, Mark Edward, and James Kirby Martin. *Drinking in America: A History.* New York: The Free Press, 1987.

– Malhotra, Richa. "Our ancestors were drinking alcohol before they were human." BBC.com, February 23, 2017.

– Marryat, Frederick. *A Diary in America: With Remarks on Its Institutions.* Second Series. Philadelphia, PA: T. K. & P. G. Collins, 1840.

– "The Martini Story," City of Martinez website.

– Matus, Victorino. *Vodka: How a Colorless, Odorless, Flavorless Spirit Conquered America.* Lanham, MD: Lyons Press, July 2014.

– McGovern, Patrick et al. "Early Neolithic wine of Georgia in the South Caucasus." *Proceedings of the National Academy of Sciences of the United States of America* 114, no. 48 (November 28, 2017).

– Messenger, Robert. "The Cocktail Renaissance." *Weekly Standard* (Washington, D.C.), August 3, 2009.

– Mitenbuler, Reid. *Bourbon Empire: The Past and Future of America's Whiskey.* New York: Penguin Books, 2016.

– Montgomery, David J. *Professor Cocktail's Zombie Horde: Recipes for the World's Most Lethal Drink.* Scotts Valley, CA: CreateSpace Independent Publishing Platform, 2013.

– Morley, Jefferson. *Snow-Storm in August: The Struggle for American Freedom and Washington's Race Riot of 1835.* New York: Anchor Books, 2013.

– Okrent, Daniel. *Last Call: The Rise and Fall of Prohibition.* New York: Scribner, 2011.

– Pace, Antonio, trans. and ed. *Luigi Castiglioni's Viaggio: Travels in the United States of North America, 1785–87.* Syracuse, NY: Syracuse University Press, 1983.

– Parsons, Brad Thomas. *Bitters: A Spirited History of a Classic Cure-All, with Cocktails, Recipes, and Formulas.* Emeryville, CA: Ten Speed Press, 2011.

– Peck, Garrett. *Prohibition in Washington, D.C.: How Dry We Weren't.* Stroud, U.K.: The History Press, 2011.

– Regan, Gary. "The Birth of the Cosmopolitan." Gazregan.com, November 30, 2012.

– Rorabaugh, W. J. *The Alcoholic Republic: An American Tradition.* New York: Oxford University Press, 1979.

– Schwartzkopf, Stacey, and Kathryn E. Sampeck, ed. *Substance and Seduction: Ingested Commodities in Early Modern Mesoamerica.* Austin, TX: University of Texas Press, 2017.

– Simonson, Robert. "How Pegu Club Forever Changed the Cocktail Game." *Grub Street*, April 7, 2015.

– *The Old Fashioned: The Story of the World's First Classic Cocktail with Recipes & Lore.* Emeryville, CA: Ten Speed Press, 2014.

– *A Proper Drink: The Untold Story of How a Band of Bartenders Saved the Civilized Drinking World.* Ten Speed Press: 2016.

– Sismondo, Christine. *America Walks*

into a Bar: A Spirited History of Taverns and Saloons, Speakeasies and Grog Shops. New York: Oxford University Press, 2014.

– Sullivan, John Jeremiah. "America's Ancient Cave Art." *Slate*, March 2011.

– Thomas, Jerry. *The Bar-Tenders' Guide: How to Mix Drinks: Or, The Bon Vivant's Companion.* New York: Dick & Fitzgerald, Publishers, 1862.

– Weightman, Gavin. *The Frozen Water Trade: A True Story.* New York: Hachette Books, 2004.

– Wheeler, Charles V. *The Life and Letters of Henry William Thomas, Mixologist.* 1926.

– Will-Weber, Mark. *Mint Juleps with Teddy Roosevelt: The Complete History of Presidential Drinking.* Washington, D.C: Regnery Publishing, 2014.

– Wondrich, David. "Ancient Mystery Revealed! The Real History (Maybe) of How The Cocktail Got Its Name *Saveur*, January 14, 2018.

– "The Coming of the Martini: An Annotated Timeline." *Daily Beast*, March 30, 2018.

– "The Cunningest Compounders of Beverages: The Hidden History of African-Americans Behind the Bar." *The Bitter Southerner*, 2018.

– "Five Unheralded Pioneers of the American Bar Who Pre-Date 'Professor' Jerry Thomas." *Eater*, May 6, 2015.

– *Imbibe! From Absinthe Cocktail to Whiskey Smash, a Salute in Stories and Drinks to "Professor" Jerry Thomas,*

Pioneer of the American Bar. Rev. ed. New York: TarcherPerigee, 2015.

– "Is Peach Brandy the Next Hot Spirit?" *Daily Beast*, December 13, 2016.

– "Masters of Mixology: William Schmidt." Liquor.com, January 19, 2011.

– *Punch: The Delights (and Dangers) of the Flowing Bowl.* New York: TarcherPerigee, 2010.

– "San Francisco's Deep Cocktail Roots." *Daily Beast*, March 20, 2018.

– "Why Did It Take America So Long to Have Female Bartenders?" *Daily Beast*, March 13, 2018.

ACKNOWLEDGMENTS

First and foremost, I would like to thank my book agent, Howard Yoon, and editor, Caitlin Leffel, for bearing with me as my ideas developed and helping to shape the final product. This book would not exist without either of you. Also, a thank-you to Rizzoli for offering me the chance to write something that has been brewing inside me for over a decade.

I would like to thank my coauthor, Bob Yule, who is not only a collaborator and dear friend but a talented historian and writer as well. It was your hard work in weaving our stories together and speaking in one voice that led to the book feeling cohesive. I am also thankful to Tim Plant for cheering us along.

My gratitude goes out to Charlotte Heal for her amazing art direction and patience in dealing with me, a visual idiot. The final result is brilliant. And to Tegan Hendel for her illustrations—I know they will be well admired.

It is important to acknowledge the people who carry you on their backs, especially while they are still carrying you. My partners at Drink Company—Angie Fetherston, JP Fetherston, Paul Taylor, and Johnny Spero—have all done so during the time I wrote this book; for their support, I am grateful, as well as for their many talents that continue to unfold.

However, even the helper needs help and support never falls on one person alone, so I am grateful to all my friends, associates, and partners of my partners for pitching in, especially Adriana Salame-Aspiazu, Maria Aspiazu, Annabelle Nebel, Coqui Aspiazu, Alex Aspiazu, Mike Burnside, Kiki Fox, Matt Fox, Chelsea Heltai, Mckenzie Harper, Alisa Cohen, Edie Burns, Alexis Spero, Gráinne Fetherston, Martin Fetherston, Éamonn Fetherston, and Kaitlynn Taylor.

I am also grateful to my former partners and associates who helped start my first bar and kept on it: Tom Brown, Nick Brown, Paul Ruppert, and Alex Bookless. Also a thank-you to Brie Husted, whose memory is still with us through the bars and restaurants she designed.

Thank you to all the head bartenders of the Columbia Room for helping my dreams come true: Katie Nelson, Matt Ficke, JP Fetherston, Suzy Critchlow, and interim head bartenders Tyler Hudgens and Mel Bowdish. You all are exemplary bartenders. And thank you to Brian Miller, who designed Columbia Room 2.0 and has been a constant friend.

Let me not leave out all the guests and regulars on whom I tested many of these stories over time. It is incredible to think how many people I have met and how they have been, however shortly, part of my life. I cannot thank you enough for supporting us and passing through.

I am eternally grateful to Babs Pinette, Jordan Zappala, Patrick Madden, Caneil McDonald, Bruce Busted, David Ferriero, and the staff of the National Archives and National Archives Foundation for including me in Spirited Republic, supporting my seminar series, and naming me Chief Spirits Advisor. What we accomplished together was the well of this book.

Thank you to all those who spoke at the History of the Cocktail seminars: David Suro-Piñera, Steve Olson, Dale DeGroff, David Wondrich, Ted Haigh, Julie Reiner, Robert Hess, Logan Ward, Steve Bashore, JP Fetherston, Wayne Curtis, Ryan Magarian,

Paul Clarke, Svetlana Legetic, Sean Kenyon, Colin Asare-Appiah, Tony Abou-Ganim, Camper English, M. Carrie Allen, Fritz Hahn, Bridget Albert, Simon Ford, Jeff "Beachbum" Berry, Jackson Cannon, Pamela Wiznitzer, Robert Simonson, Garrett Peck, Duane Sylvestre, Talia Baiocchi, and Victor Matus. You each contributed time and knowledge to the series and guided my understanding of the cocktail's history and relevance. I can think of no more esteemed group of experts.

Thank you to all the members and founders of the DC Craft Bartenders Guild. Whatever small contribution I made to its inception has been eclipsed by your work, and I am thrilled to see so many members and people impacted by a simple idea to bring committed bartenders together to help each other, especially Gina Chersevani, who took my call when I had this crazy idea.

Thank you to Phil Greene, a mentor and friend, who helped launch my career and to all the past and present board members of the Museum of the American Cocktail for including me among your ranks, especially Jill DeGroff and Laura McMillian.

There are so many bartending, hospitality, and spirits friends to thank, and I am sure I will miss some. I want you all to know how much it meant to have your friendship, help, and support. Thank you to Sother Teague, Jeffrey Morgenthaler, Eryn Reece, Elba Giron, Bill Thomas, Eric Seed, Jake Parrot, Michael Lowe, John Uselton, Scott and Becky Harris, Chad Robinson, Clyde Davis, Melanie Asher, Lynnette Marrero, Ivy Mix, Tess Mix, Alexandre Gabriel, Guillaume Lamy, Julio Cabrera, Alex Day, Dave Kaplan, Michelle Bernstein, Ron Cooper, Bryan Tetorakis, Trevor Frye, Todd Thrasher, Devin Gong, Jon Arroyo, Rachel Sergi, Jeff Faile, Rico Wisner, Dan Searing, Juan Coronado, Phoebe Easmon, Christian Gaul, Misty Kalkofen, Ryan Maybee, and those who passed from untimely deaths: Rob Cooper and John Lermayer. A very special thank you to Chantal Tseng, who was instrumental in learning and growing in the craft with me.

I am incredibly thankful to the team at Beverage Alcohol Resource. Their mentorship and support has been invaluable to helping me learn and build my career.

Thank you to my mom, who so rarely drank at home that I was naturally curious, and for giving me life, twice. I also thank my father for having the courage to confront his own demons and help so many others cross the bridge. I thank my brothers and sisters for enduring my endless snobbery, annoyingness, and occasional reclusiveness. and my godchildren, Mia and Halcyon, who are always in my prayers.

Thank you to my son for being the most exceptional part of my life and giving me more joy than I could ever imagine, and to his mother, Kim, who put up with more than anyone should and has given more than most people can.

Thank you to my dearest friends Ben Eisendrath, Damon Fodge, Stephane Muszynski, Adam Bernbach, Glenn Burns, and Father Bill Dailey for encouragement and support. Friendship is the only true reason for drinking; it both deepens one's love and softens the passing of time.

Thank you to Maria Bastasch for your love, support, and patience while I finished my book.

In 2019, we live in difficult times, when it is not easy to acknowledge the source of our world and the many wonderful things in it. Yet I would be remiss in not mentioning my faith and how it affected my views on bartending, drinking, and hospitality: I thank Jesus Christ for unceasing love and mercy and the truest joy in my life, which is to cleave to God.

Lastly, thank you to the gift of drinking and, especially, to the wisdom to know when to put the bottle down. G. K. Chesterton said it best: "Never drink because you need it, for this is rational drinking, and the way to death and hell. But drink because you do not need it, for this is irrational drinking, and the ancient health of the world."

DEDICATION

To Angie for your encouragement, inspiration, and support and because a drink is only as good as the company you share. — DEREK

To my parents James and Elizabeth Yule, my grandmothers Mary Quayle and Brittie Yule, and my husband, Tim Plant, the ultimate drinking companion. — BOB

First published in the United States of America in 2019 by Rizzoli International Publications, Inc. 300 Park Avenue South, New York, NY 10010
www.rizzoliusa.com
© 2018 Derek Brown
Foreword text © David S. Ferriero

All rights reserved. No part of this publication may be reproduced, stored in a retrieval system, or transmitted in any form or by any means, electronic, mechanical, photocopying, recording, or otherwise, without prior consent of the publishers.

2019 2020 2021 2022/ 10 9 8 7 6 5 4 3 2 1
Distributed in the U.S trade by Random House, New York.
Designed by Charlotte Heal Design
Text written by Derek Brown and Bob Yule
Illustrations by Tegan Hendel
Rizzoli editor: Caitlin Leffel
Printed in China
ISBN: 978-0-8478-6146-0
Library of Congress Control Number: 2018960902